# BECOMING
# THE CREATOR

## A PRACTICAL GUIDE TO
## SPIRITUALITY AND CONNECTION

# DAOSITH LEMAY

MINDSTIR MEDIA

Published by Mindstir Media, LLC
45 Lafayette Rd | Suite 181 | North Hampton, NH 03862 | USA
1.800.767.0531 | www.mindstirmedia.com

Printed in the United States of America
ISBN-13: 978-1-7376287-9-8

# CONTENTS

# PREFACE

All that I unveil unto you are my life experiences and my beliefs. These beliefs are my own and mine alone. This is my truth. It does not mean it is yours. I am merely giving my perspective and it is your own free will to accept it as truth or not. Of course, it does not have to be absolute truth either. One thing is for sure, we are always adjusting our beliefs in a constantly changing continuum. You must use YOUR OWN DISCERNMENT. Take what resonates with you. Leave the rest.

I do not believe in coincidences. Accepting the idea of coincidences would suggest that the synchronicities that I experienced throughout my life were just random byproducts of life or nature. The notion of coincidences being a byproduct of nature is an oxymoron to me. For everything I see in nature has specific intention, whether we know it or not. The intention is there, and I see the Universe arranging itself to meet that intention.

Life blooms with intention. You can find geometric shapes and the Fibonacci sequence throughout nature repeatedly. Throughout nature, life matches with its surroundings. These things do not happen by accident and they are not by coincidence. It is by intention that life adapts and flourishes. Life wants to be seen and we find it everywhere. Even when humanity believes life could not exist, we discover that it does. New species are found every year in the same places and in new places. There are more discoveries of life showing how little we know about the nature of our world. It is showing us how interwoven life is. We are part of life force and there is intention behind every experience whether you believe it or not. It is like a divine architect is working behind the scenes.

There are intentions behind every life, even yours and mine. My life began in a very fluid state. I say that because I am not one hundred percent certain about the accuracy of my birth information. I only have a few memories, some documents with contradicting information, and information handed to me over the years. I was born to a Laotian mother, Keo, and a Chinese father, Sone. My biological parents were refugees escaping the Laos killing fields by the communist Khmer Rouge regime. My father and mother, who was pregnant with me at the time, fled their home and managed to get into a refugee camp in Ubon, Thailand. It was there I made my entry into the world.

My parents managed to immigrate into the Unites States via San Francisco when I was about one year old. At some point, we transitioned over to New England and landed somewhere in the state of Rhode Island. My brother was born during the transition from San Francisco to Rhode Island.

My early core years with my biological parents were filled with difficult experiences. Sone was an abusive father who drank frequently. My mother was suffering from a mental illness and physical health issues. My memories from those times are full of feeling unsafe, betrayed, hurt, abused, pain, and a lack of love. I was in a constant state of fear. I was usually alone. There are not too many loving memories in general, neither from my mother or my father. There was constant turmoil between my parents. Arguments and fights that carried over to my brother and I. Physical punishment was common. Sone would hit me with many different household items, such as belts, coat hangers, broomsticks, etc. . . . If physical abuse was not enough, he would lock me in a room without the ability to use the bathroom. Food was scarce and monetary lack were constant themes. I recall my brother having a malnourished pot belly and I was always hungry. We slept on used mattresses on the floor and wore clothes given to us.

We moved to Laconia, New Hampshire, at some point. My parents were sponsored through a Lutheran church service along with twenty or so other immigrating Lao families. We bounced around different locations in Laconia. I began my early education at Woodland Heights Elementary School.

It was soon after, on one fateful night, my mother, brother, and I left my father. I am not sure of the circumstances, but we found ourselves at a Salvation Army facility. Child services was brought in, and we were removed from my mother's custody. This is where my brother and I began our experience in foster care.

My brother and I became part of the New Hampshire foster care program. We moved around within the New Hampshire Lakes Region, mostly staying around Laconia, with just the clothes on our backs and what little belongings we had in small trash bags. My brother and I spent time at several different homes until we arrived at the Lemay family. It would be with the Lemay family that a new chapter would begin in my life.

Greg and Lauren Lemay had three children of their own. Adding my brother and I to the mix made it a full house of seven. Greg was dealing with fallout from a family business going bankrupt and Lauren was an educator at Woodland Heights Elementary School in Laconia. The Lemays brought another level of family dynamic to my reality. Although my brother and I felt more settled and safer, there was still some common themes that carried over. Lack and self-worth issues continued to repeat.

The rest of my childhood and adolescence would be considered normal compared to my earlier years. I was a C or B average student and played sports. I enjoyed being with friends and mostly was part of jock cliques. Sports provided me with much of my self-worth and confidence. It was also an outlet for a lot of my anger. I dealt with a lot of anger growing up and most of it was directed toward my brother. We had many fights that led to physical confrontations and pain. Most of it was about being angry because he would not listen to me.

After high school, I went to the University of New Hampshire for my undergrad. I graduated from the business school and went into the financial planning industry. I developed my business sense over those years and found that I liked working with people the most. I enjoyed the face-to-face interactions and getting to know clients.

The first firm I was with was a large institution. There were many different learning experiences with that firm. After a few years, I decided to join a smaller New Hampshire based financial planning firm as an advisor. I spent the next ten years at that firm and became a partner. We later sold that firm to a much larger firm. By that time I was earning six figures and was feeling more secure in my finances.

I met my wife during my transition to the smaller firm. We dated for several years. We got married in 2013 and began a family shortly after. The birth of my daughter was the catalyst to my spiritual awakening. It opened me up and forced me to dive further into the spiritual world. I accredit her for putting me on my true purpose and the beginning of my journey. Her birth began a chain of events of inner searching and healing that brought me to where I am today. It was a crash course in remembering who I was and what I am.

Most of my past dealt with patterns of anger and running away from pain. Trying to control my life, not to feel buried emotions, and keeping my environment safe. It was a constant battle of feeling powerless since I felt like a victim. I did what I could to not feel the pain of rejection and not being loved. There was a lot of anger, and I was easily triggered by things that would seem ridiculous to an outsider. I spent much of my time protecting myself from these things. I was projecting an image to the outside world of something that was not true. It was because I did not believe I was good enough as my true self.

I share my experiences with you to offer you a pathway to healing, empowerment, and oneness that is the culmination of the last few decades of my life. I say *a pathway* because it is not the only way. In the ad infinitum, it is one variation, one expression of healing and way of being. This has been my permission slip for myself to work through my traumas and to become more centered and peaceful. I hope that this body of work, the energy that fills these pages, provides you a practical way of loving yourself. A practical way to approach your own spirituality and finding connection with all things, especially with yourself. May this guide help you feel more grounded and connected to your life in a way that is deeply rewarding. One where you experience life changing results and become the creator that you are.

This information, which is vibrational in nature, will provide what is needed to you based on your own vibrational state of being. It is thrust upon you to decide how you want to interpret and utilize the information. My hope is you utilize this guide for accessing your divine self and for your highest good. My hope is it catalyzes you to empower yourself to look inward and find the truth of who you are. Have courage, my friend, to offer yourself love and rediscover everything you have forgotten. To recollect the pieces of you that you have given away and reclaim the truth that you are Source, and you are always, always loved.

And so it is.

# CHAPTER 1:
# YOU ARE THE CREATOR

*"You are a meteor crashed into the earth and
shattered into many fragments."*

*– Spiritual Guide*

I woke up from a dream in the early morning hours. My energy was elevated, and my heart was pumping rapidly. I felt like I could jump out of bed and run a marathon. The dream was so clear and vivid to me that I had to make sure that I was not still dreaming. I looked over to see my wife was still sleeping. I directed my attention to myself and focused on my breath. I quickly grabbed my dream journal and wrote down everything I could remember.

My guide had visited me in my dream. This was happening more often, but this time was different. She taught me things and delivered messages. What she expressed to me were details regarding my experience entering into this dimension, into my earthly incarnation. She said to me, "You are a meteor, crashed into earth and shattered into many fragments." I jumped with excitement in my eureka moment. Her metaphor resonated with me on so many levels and so deeply within me that I knew it to be true. I replied to her, "Aha! That is me! That is exactly how I feel!" She then began to share and show all sorts of information to me.

Our interaction was one of many different experiences that we would continue to have. She, along with many other guides both physical and non-physical, have certainly offered insight into the reality in which we engage in. Insight into how things work and why they work. Something that many people never bother to ask nor investigate.

My life experiences have been widows and doorways to worlds that have been hidden. These worlds are deep within you and many of us are fearful to look at them. I have used my own experiences and that which is shared to me by others to understand more about who I am. To know more about the truth of what you and I are. I share my own spiritual path in hopes to offer insight as to why your life is the way it is and that you choose it for yourself. I share this so you may remember your true self and the natural way of your being. It is a natural state of being of empowerment, love, wholeness, and connection to Source. A path filled with more love, more joy, and more awareness of self. A journey back home and becoming the creator.

What you are about to embark on is a journey, a quest of sorts. Like a warrior in a video game, starting out with little power or little knowledge of the known world or the journey ahead. You will venture into new places, meet new people, discover new knowledge, and engage in dark battles of which you have never imagined. All whilst attaining new power and uncovering your truth. Do not be fooled though, this quest is not for the fainthearted. You will be tested. You will want to avoid things, run from things, and reject what you see. It will be the hardest thing you will ever do. There will be days you will want to quit and give up. You will want to tuck your tail and run. But you will not. For you cannot imagine going back to the way you were. You will forge forward because you know there is truth to be found.

You will not give up. For when those days come, you will find the strength to move forward. You will confront your fears and dive into the opportunity that lay before you. For those with enough courage and bravery to continue, the path will find immeasurable wealth. Those that walk this path cannot imagine life any other way. It becomes their way of life. For the warrior knows no other way but to face their fears and battle through. For each step brings the warrior closer to the secrets of life and the truth. Yes, you will overcome and be renewed in your willpower, your strength, and your resolve.

This is a journey to recollect the fragments of you. Fragments of the powerful you that were given away. It is a wonderful journey to reclaim the truth of who you are. You will rediscover the fragments of yourself lost in the illusions of separation. Removing these illusions of who you are based on limitations and false identities will unveil your true power that has always been there. For the action of removing illusions and reclaiming your power are one in the same. The more you reclaim your power the more your false illusions fade. When your illusions are stripped from your earthly being, you will find the authentic self. The authentic self is the treasure, it is the truth. The truth of who is the rightful ruler upon the throne. Take up the challenge as the warrior and become what you were meant to be. The true ruler.

You will reclaim your ownership of the throne. You will remember you are the true ruler of your own kingdom as a sovereign, joyous, and loving being. For you are the rightful, divinely anointed to sit upon the throne as the golden one. To do so, you must remember what you are. You must remember what you lost. This is a journey; this is a path.

## MY SPIRITUAL AWAKENING

I started to look at my life differently in 2016. Perhaps that is why you are reading this guide. You are feeling a nudge and believe there is more to life. You are starting to look at life differently and questioning your purpose. You feel something inside you calling out to something and do not know what it is, and that is why you are searching. Whatever led you here, know it was by no accident. It was not by coincidence that you decided to put your energy into finding this book and read through it. It was by vibrational match to something inside you, otherwise it would not have shown up in your reality. You are awakening to what you truly are. This was the same for me.

I always thought that there was more to life than just a material existence. I felt life should be more than just working day in and day out to fulfill your worldly material desires. The desires formulated through what I saw in all the media outlets. Images and projections of materialistic experiences such as having a nice big house, driving a fancy car, traveling all over the world, drinking champagne on a yacht, and all the financial success one could ask for. Everyone else was following along, but something just did not fit with me. It felt like it was fake. It felt like it was all a show. It was like being in a factory line and seeing people doing the same things over and over. Time and time again, I found that those things brought only temporary happiness and fulfillment. It left me with many unanswered questions. Questions about my purpose and what I was doing. In addition, I was repeating the same old stories in my life. I was getting tired of being angry and exploding over simple arguments. I was tired of feeling like a victim and blaming others for what was going wrong. I remember saying to myself, *There's got to be a better way. I don't want to feel this way anymore.*

I spent years feeling angry because I was holding on to so much pain and hurt. I was projecting my anger at family and friends. My closest family relationship got the brunt of that anger. In my childhood, my brother was on the receiving end of many fistfights, verbal attacks, and out of control anger because he would not listen to me. I wanted control and when he did not listen it turned into physical confrontations. I was trying to feel powerful and anger was the solution. Later in life, my wife became aware of all my trauma hidden inside me. There were constant patterns replaying in our relationship. It was always someone else's fault, not my own. I was a victim and felt powerless. I would turn to violence; I would emotionally shut down or numb myself from feeling. These emotions made me want to physically leave. I wanted to be anywhere but there. I dealt with self-worth issues throughout my life too.

I wanted approval and validation. I worked hard as an athlete during my high school years. I focused primarily on soccer as my source of confidence and self-worth. I constantly practiced drills to improve my skills. I wanted to be seen as a star to my team and to the public. There were a lot of anger and self-worth issues whenever I did not perform to my expectations or was not involved in scoring goals.

I was desperate for a girlfriend during those years. I wanted to be wanted. I wanted to be loved. Romantic relationships were never truly deep connections, but rather a need to fulfill my self-worth. Most relationships were superficial and remained at a physical level because I did not want to fully commit. In some cases that turned into hurtful relationships or short-lived sexual experiences.

I drank alcohol and I did drugs. It was all part of my social environment, but it was also a way for me to escape my reality. It was a way to escape my pain and the repressed emotions inside of me. Another way I escaped my pain was video games. I would spend hours playing video games and attach to the screen. This carried on until my early 30s.

It was in 2016 when my first child was born. She cracked me open like an egg. Something inside me shifted. It was a driving force and a relentless feeling to search for something. I began reading all sorts of self-help books and spiritual books. I turned inward and began a regime of meditation. I would try to meditate whenever I could. It was then I began to sense energies and certain things in my meditative space. I began a search for explanations for things, like seeing colors around people. I met with many different psychics, mediums, and spiritually open people to find some clarity in my life.

What I found was past traumas were keeping me from moving forward in my life. I was holding on to things that needed to be healed. It became apparent to me when I was asked about my mother during a meeting. The second I was asked about my mother I broke down and I could not control my emotions. I began to sob uncontrollably. I knew then, there was pain and I had been hiding it within me. It needed to heal.

This sent me further into my inner seeking. I increased the time I spent in my meditation searching for answers. During my mediations I would revisit memories about my life. Memories of my mother and father. I would relive each experience in my meditative state and explore what had happened. I explored as many memories as possible that I could find with the stored energy of my trauma and pain. I inquired about the patterns around feeling like a powerless victim, feeling unloved, feeling unsafe, and feeling unworthy. It was in those meditative states that I began to see how things came to be for me. I understood I never took accountability for what I went through. That I was an unconsciously living my life and recreating the same patterns.

I was unconscious of myself. It was like I was on autopilot. I was missing a lot of things moving through life unconscious. I was missing all the red flags and warning signs showing up everywhere. I was missing the opportunity to change. I was missing opportunities to love myself and make choices of empowerment. These patterns of anger were all opportunities to heed the call from deep within and to heal and find happiness. The calls came from somewhere beyond this physical place. It called me to walk a path inward and to start healing. To start finding joy in my life again.

I spent a good amount of my life avoiding myself. My emotions were being invalidated by me. I was rejecting and denying them because they did not feel good to me. All the anger, pain, hurt, suffering, and sadness was being rejected. I refused to acknowledge them, and I was hardly at peace within myself. I wanted to be something other than what I was because being me was not good enough.

There was an energy that was nudging and trying to show me a different way. It was trying to awaken me from my sleep. It was trying to show me how I gave pieces of myself away. It was my soul, the spark of Source, that wanted me to look inward to find the answers. To find what needed to be seen and to seek the answers inside of me. Inside me was where I found my answers to who, what, where, why, and how. Within myself was the truth and the path to becoming the creator.

## THE CREATOR: THERE IS INTENTION IN EVERYTHING

On my family's property in New Hampshire, the night sky was clear enough to see the stars. With deep focus in your eyes and a bit of imagination, you could make out the silhouette of the Milky Way Galaxy. I would stare with wonder at our galaxy and wonder about the beauty of the unknown. It is an awe-inspiring view.

I have always been fond of the stars in the night sky. There is so much to marvel at. So much wonder about the existence of it all. There is terrific excitement to imagine all the different worlds and places. It all led me to ask, how could such things be created? How can there be such beauty? At the same time, I would feel frustrated by it. I would be frustrated that we know so little. I was frustrated by humanity's limited perspective about our existence. Why do humans believe that we are not part of all of this? When we look up at the stars or the vastness of the Universe, or even at the beauty of our own planet, many believe they are removed from it. Many believe that they are not part of it but separate from it. Like we are an error or mistake that does not belong. Separated out from the beauty and love of Source.

From my perspective, humanity is deeply connected to this beauty. We are part of the reason, and the reason is part of us. There is a relationship to our being with everything that we see. There is intention in our reality that exists all around us, which you and I are part of. What you decide to call this soup of a Universe is up to you. Be it Source, Creator, All That There Is, The Great Unknown, The Great Spirit, etc. It exists all around you and you are part of it. I choose not to expand on the word "God." This is partly because of how the word has been humanized a bit. The intention we experience in our external reality comes from Source. What I hope to share with you is that Source is also within you, just as it is everywhere else. You are part of this world much like anything else you see in your reality and beyond. Nothing more and nothing less, but part of it all.

There are countless stories about Source or the Universe. I read and heard stories about people telling others what they think Source is. Any religion will say to you that Source is all things. Source created everything. Source is the smallest particles to the incomprehensible size of galaxies and beyond. Source is everywhere. It is everywhere and everything and all the stuff in between, except within you. All the stories we hear about is always about you being outside of Source. Source is in everywhere and everything but within you.

Most people believe that they are cast outside of Source. Why would Source create everything and be everything, but *NOT* within you? Why are you not part of that Source? Like there was an agreement that everything is good, but humans are bad. I have an issue with this perspective. It is a contradiction to say the least. Why is Source everywhere but not within you? Why are we told that? Source exists in all things and it is the Universe we experience, yet we humans believe we are cast out from Source's bosom. In some religions, we are cast out as unworthy from birth and must prove our worth to Source. This feels like a linear and humanized depiction of Source that is extremely limiting. One that depicts an all-loving and powerful being that created the known Universe but has the human characteristics of holding a grudge against something. The idea does not vibrationally match.

The idea that Source is outside of us would imply we are lower than and we are powerless. It is like we are subservient and powerless to the omnipotent power that be. I would vehemently disagree with this. We are powerful and we are equal. We are more powerful than we know.

There are more times than not that humanity has proven how powerful it is. Against all the odds humans, both individually and collectively, have proven that our wills, thoughts, beliefs, and actions can achieve anything. Humans have created unbelievable things and it all started with us. We have built cities, created all sorts of music and arts, pushed the human body to unbelievable limits, gone into space, etc., you name it, we are doing it. We have shown tremendous power to overcome obstacles and move forward as a species. All because we have the power to create.

Where does your power come from? Have you ever asked that question? It comes from somewhere, but where? How are you able to even exist? Your power all comes from Source, and you exist because of Source. If you existed outside of Source you would not exist. How are you able to move through the day with thoughts and actions? How did your life come into existence? It is my belief that you are the reason life happens. You are not separate from this world. You are not separate from Source. You are very much indeed part of the vastness that makes up this Universe. You are integral to the relationship that makes this world go round. This is because you are made from it.

The best place to start is from the beginning. In the beginning there was Source. Source is all knowing and is all. There was only Source with its immeasurable spirit. Source, being all-knowing and everything, had a desire. A desire to fulfill a material understanding of itself because it was only of spirit. That desire manifested the material Universes that we experience today. Source created our Universe through sheer spiritual force to fulfill its material desire to know itself.

Within that desire to know itself, it birthed infinitesimal replications of itself. These infinitesimal sparks of Source were created from itself. These sparks of Source were to experience and fulfill the desire of Source to know itself. These sparks of Source expanded on that material desire. Your soul, that resides within you, is but a fractal of the one and infinite Source creator. A piece of all that is and ever will be. You are a fragment of that ever knowing and loving Source. Birth from love within love. You are fractal, but you are also whole. You are whole in that your soul was given all the creative powers akin to that of the one infinite Source. You are fractal in that you are only a piece of Source. You cannot be less than or more than what you are because you are Source. You are everything and all, but you are a fragment. This is a paradox. It is a paradox that you will become more aware of as you move forward in your spiritual journey and healing. Our lives are full of paradoxes, and this is because we are a paradox. You are Source, all knowing and all things, seeking to know itself through the fragment of Source that is you. Why does an all-knowing being seek to understand itself? The answer is because you are asking. Quite a paradox.

You are a fragmentation of Source expanding your energy to understand yourself. You, as part of Source, have created all that is before your eyes. You are experiencing yourself through what you know as life. This is all a co-creation with other Source fragments to know yourself as Source. All of this is but a co-creation of your powerful spark to experience what you are like. To know what it is to be Source through the soup that we understand as the Universe and the material expressions before us. We are the desire of Source to help it understand itself.

I can sense a cataclysm of sorts from those who read this under the limited doctrine of the world's religions. Take a moment not to throw this information out just because it is bucking against your religious beliefs. If you were willing to read this information up until now, be open to what I am willing to share.

My intention is not to uproot your personal beliefs around your religion. My intention is to open your neurological pathways to a different perspective that might offer more peace in your life than what you have experienced thus far.

Much of the religious dogma is about an all-loving creator that cherishes *His* creations, but in the same line of text would hold a grudge against you until your worth is proven. What hypocrisy is that? What all-loving creator would create something only to turn around and cast that creation into the abyss? Then hold a grudge against you until you proved yourself?! That is humanizing and linearizing something that is beyond our comprehension. It is humanizing something that is beyond space and time.

My truth is that Source is within you. It is as simple as that. Is the simple idea that we are Source so foolish and unrealistic to so many people? Is it that far of a stretch to believe that you are part of Source? Or have we been so indoctrinated to think so lowly of ourselves that we could never be a part of Source? In my mind, this perspective or this truth explains why we have so much contrast in our world.

Why does there exist such turmoil in the world? Why does there exist such hatred and unfairness in the world, if there is an all-loving Source? Let us look at the phrase of "all-loving." Is not the term itself to be loving to all? All-loving is unconditional love, there is not favoritism. It is to accept in its entirety that which it is witnesses to. To express Source with humanized traits, liking holding grudges against people for their choices or to say they are favored, seems out of alignment with "all-loving." We must move beyond the humanized version or definitions projected onto us. We must move beyond definitions that further humanize Source and create more separation and divisiveness. We must remove the belief that we are less than and powerless. In my perspective, we are made of Source. We are Source and we chose to have these experiences because we want to experience them. It is because we are Source, and we create this dysfunction.

We have all these outrageous experiences because Source allows it. We, as humanity, created hatred, war, crime, suffering, and all the turmoil in this world. We chose it and we are the ones creating it. There is no one else making us do it. Humanity chooses to use its creative power to expand on all this turmoil. We are allowed to because we are Source seeking to understand itself as Source. Why would Source stop itself from knowing itself? Source will not interfere and does not interfere because Source is all-loving for itself. We believe we are separate from everything and therefore are allowed to experience all this turmoil. Source will help us to expand on the belief of separation.

Within you is a spark with the same power to create as Source. You are given the right to create and expand your energy so that you can understand yourself. This is where your power comes from. It comes from within, put there by Source to know itself. Therefore, your power to create and manifest realities is given. You create realities with your intention of thoughts, beliefs, and actions. You are creating your reality to experience yourself as Source. It does not mean you consciously want it, but at some level you are creating to experience these things through your life. This is my truth as to why we experience so much contrast and turmoil. This is a truth to understand why things are the way they are in your life. It is an empowered perspective.

When humanity can anchor this empowered consciousness, it may find more unity and connection in the world. We would create knowing that we are all the same energy, and this may lead to a world vastly different than what we are experiencing now. It does not mean we need to be homogenous in our experience or expression of who we are, it just means we can connect on a higher level. A higher level beyond just our human self. A higher level that offers healing, connection, sovereignty, and love.

Currently, humanity feels separate because you feel separated. You believe you are separated from Source because you feel separated within yourself. You are separated by an illusion. It is an illusion that keeps you outside and different. We spin endless stories about ourselves because of fear. The illusion creates repressed emotions, traumas, and limited beliefs that keep you small and disempowered. It is your limited belief that keeps you where you are and cut off from the love that is all around you. Our beliefs are blocking us from becoming what we are meant to be, beloved creators. It may be time to look at what you define as Source and see if you have outgrown that belief.

Scientists claim that we are all made up of the same materials that existed at the beginning of the Universe. If Source is everything that you see, then would it not make sense to say that we are also made up of the same things? We are made of star dust. The same star dust and materials that made our solar system, our galaxy, and beyond. That star dust is within us. The planets, the sun, and everything else we can see as we stare into the vastness of our starry night sky are all tied together through the same material and energy. It is the same star dust that existed from the beginning of our Universe and will continue to be around until the end, if there is one. In that simple and profound idea, you and I are all that there is and ever was. We are the Universe, and the Universe is us. You are Source and Source is you. It cannot be anything less or more. You are the same and can manifest into reality all that you desire.

Let us take another example. In thermal dynamics, there is concept called the law of conservation. It states that energy cannot be created or destroyed.

What that means is that energy can only be transferred or transformed from one form to another. For example, let us imagine a solid piece of wood on fire. The solid piece of wood is made of a standing energy wave that seems like a solid state. The elements or atomic molecules making up that piece of wood are vibrating in a certain molecular pattern. Now we add the element of fire. As fire burns the wood, the energy within the wood begins to transmute into different forms. There is a chemical reaction, and it turns into heat, it turns into light, it turns into smoke, and the wood becomes coal that will become ashes. The ashes will return to the earth and be used for the soil. Then the energy is recycled for whatever use it is deemed for next. The energy never gets destroyed. It never disappears or goes away. It just becomes something different; it transforms into another energy.

If energy has never been created or destroyed, then we are the same energy that has been around since the Big Bang, or what scientist claim is the start of this Universe. Our energy has been around since the beginning of our Universe and it will be around for the next billions of years or infinity thereafter. We have the same energy within us that created the Universe. We are the same energy as the Universe. The stars that we are in awe of in the night sky are made of the same star dust and energy that makes up your entire being. Body, mind, and spirit. Ever wonder then, where did the origin of all this energy come from? It must have come from somewhere. That somewhere is Source. You are Source and Source is you.

My guides also shared with me that our experience, what we see in our reality, is light and sound vibrating at difference speeds. It is energy from Source that is separated by difference in vibration. We will dive a little more into this in the next chapter, but what you perceive in your reality is energy in standing waves of solid state based on the observer. You are experiencing Source within itself pretending to be separate from you. It is only energy moving at different speeds or vibrations.

Think about the concept of the light prism. When you shine a white light into the prism, you see the light broken out into the colors of the rainbow. That is akin to the energy we experience in our life. You are merely seeing energy fragmented and holding a different vibration from the whole. It all comes from the original Source, and it gets split out in infinite ways. Just like the colors of the rainbow that come from white light, you are from a higher original form. All you see is Source energy holding different vibrational patterns to give the illusion of separation. That also includes you. You are an aspect of Source experiencing your identity of separation from everything else. You are made of the same energy that all is made up of.

What I am trying to show you is that this is no mere idea. It is a profound change in beliefs. This is the foundation on which I found more joy and peace in my life. You ARE Source. You are as much a part of this Universe and everything within it. The same creative force that is Source is within you. You have the same power and love within you, and it makes up every cell, atom, and electron in your body. The same creative force flows through you.

As the concept concretes within your mind, perhaps the next wonder is how you have been applying your creative power. Look around your world and realize that all that you see before you is a function of your doing. It did not come to pass by accident, nor did it happen to manifest without your intention, whether you are conscious of it or not. You may not know how certain items were created but you have come to experience them in your reality through your will. The same goes for how you go about your day interacting with different people and different places. The experiences you have and how your life up until now has all been because of you.

What I am suggesting is that your consciousness, your energy, and your entire vibrational being is affecting your reality. It is dependent on how you choose to use your power. To understand that power one needs to see the results of it. For you are the creative force behind the wind and the rain. You are the answer to all your questions. It does not exist outside of you. It exists within you and through you.

Have you ever wondered where your desires originate from? Do you think they come out of thin air? What causes you or drives you to want to do this or eat that or experience certain things? Sure, there are basic needs to fulfill such as food and shelter, but what about beyond that. Where does the desire to jump out of an airplane come from? Where does the desire to create an expression of a beautiful landscape come from? Where does the desire to play music come from? To this day, many experts and scientist know little of what drives our desires or where they originate from. Your desires do not just manifest out of thin air. They come from some place. Some would say that you come preloaded with them. That begs the question, who preloaded them? The human desires are expressions of your Source connection.

The seed of you is from Source. The seed of your desires come from Source. The core to your existence is to understand yourself. It is the desire of Source that moves through you. It swells up from the infinite depth of your inner self that is Source. You are the manifested desire of Source.

Any desire you have springs forth through your being. It comes into the mind and becomes the inspiring energy for action. You, as a fragment of Source, move with the thoughts and actions to fulfill a desire. You manifest the experience through you. It is through you that you fulfill your desire and create your reality. It is through you that you seek to know yourself.

## YOU ARE THE CREATOR

It took me a long time to realize that I am accountable for my actions. I am accountable for my life. I am the one choosing my reality and all that comes with it. No one else can make you happy or make you more peaceful. If they do, it is only if they are around and that is fleeting. You must take ownership in your creations. You must be the reason why you are happy and empowered. It begins with changing your perspective on how you look at your reality.

Many of you are looking at life through a lens. It is like having a pair of sunglasses on your face the whole time. You are completely oblivious that you are wearing them. These glasses distort your vision of the world. The glasses can reduce the brightness, or block you from seeing certain colors, or even block you from seeing complete objects. There are infinite lenses to wear. Many of them are limiting.

At this juncture, I am trying to help you become aware that you are wearing sunglasses. The minute you take them off, you will notice how different things are. It will take some time to adjust to the vision. Once you adjust to the difference, you will notice how different things are and how much clearer they are. Colors are more vivid. There are incredible ranges and shades to colors, where before they would seem dull. You may be able to see things at a distance with a clearer sense. You may see details of things that you could not see before. Objects that have been hidden become obvious to the eye. It is not the outside world that changed. It is merely the action of taking off the sunglasses and seeing with your true eyes.

This shift in perspective is not a small endeavor. The creator commands reign over their kingdom and must embody it wholly. It is a practice. It is a way of being in its entirety. The practice is seeing the world as the creator. Looking and knowing that your reality is a hologram based on your intentions. You are projecting a hologram and living it. You are like an unbelievably sophisticated computer projecting onto a screen images based on your programming.

The computer is a great way to understand this further. I am not someone who is well-versed in computer technology. I honestly am only able to manage some software programs. I am only aware of the programs that I use, basically the essentials for me to do my work. Microsoft Excel, Word, email, internet searches, etc. So, beyond the few software programs that I use, I am completely unaware of the other programs, even the hardware, used to run my computer. I am not sure what is used to project images on my screen.

Most live life unaware of their programs. We go through our day without questioning the programs that are running. We do not take time to understand what other programs are causing us pain or hurt in our reality. Most people do not even question their existence. We go about our day banging our heads against the same things over and over hoping that they will solve themselves.

Albert Einstein once said, "Insanity is doing the same thing over and over and expecting different results." Insanity can also be defined as extreme foolishness and irrationality. Much of my life has been trying to fix my patterns without truly understanding why and hoping it will change. It is irrational and foolhardy to think that we can change unconscious patterns with the same thinking that got us there in the first place. We change who we are or how we think to break the pattern. We must introduce a new paradigm.

There have been countless times in my life where I felt like a victim. I was a victim when I had to spend money on my car or had to replace my septic system. I could not keep the money that I had earned not matter how hard

I tried. I found myself constantly dealing with large expenses to fix things. I would say, "Of course! Of course, this would happen! Why do these things always happen to me?!" Just like a victim, I was angry about money I was spending and continued with life with the same mindset. The pattern would continue to repeat. Nothing ever changed until I changed my understanding of what I was experiencing. I needed to see the experience through the empowered creator. It was a shift in my perspective that allowed for change. It shifted my reality and I found more abundance, love, and empowerment.

## EYES OF THE CREATOR

The mindset of the creator is an empowering process. This is because you are taking accountability for the results and actions in your life. Stepping into the "creator" you automatically step out of the role of the victim. This perspective empowers the individual to see things for what they are, simply creations of one's energy. A creation does not denote a conscious intent. It just means that you were the force that brought the creation about and you need to find some level of accountability. The creator looks upon that which has created and wonders upon it.

To move forward with more peace and happiness in your life requires the removal of disempowered beliefs. You must remove the sunglasses that place blame on the external. You must step into the role of the creator. The role of the creator will help you see answers to things that would otherwise be unseen. All that you have experienced and gone through is connected to you. In some way your life, up until now, has been your own doing. It was created through you. NO ONE ELSE. You are responsible for your life. You are the creator. The decisions you make and the way you react to your reality is your choice. This returns the power back to you. You are no longer allowing external factors to control you. The creator takes ownership of the creations.

Imagine an artist painting their canvas. They go about painting their work of art and suddenly their brush stroke goes astray. Does the artist yell and blame the canvas for the error that occurred? Does the artist blame the paint for forcing them to brush erroneously? Does the artist blame the brush for the mistake? No. It would be futile because the artist is the one in control. The artist is controlling the tools that are the brush, paint, and canvas.

When it comes to our own lives, we lose that perspective. We get lost in the story and we forget who is responsible. We go back to blaming the external world for our problems even though we are the ones creating all the pain and suffering. The Universe is not against you. It is not picking on you and making your life miserable like a bully. The Universe is working for you. You just need to take accountability and become the creator.

I was like an artist blaming his tools and not himself. It was how I lived my life. I lived in a state of victimhood. I would put the blame on other people and never take responsibility for what had occurred. I remember an experience where my wife and I were fighting after purchasing our first house together. She wanted new carpets and new paint on the walls. It was a huge trigger for me. Without understanding why, I got so angry and started yelling at her. "Nothing is ever good enough for you! You are just spending my money and doing what you want! Why can't you just be happy with what we have?! I never get any say in what we do in this house! Even if I did, it wouldn't be good enough for you!" I was fuming and pacing the kitchen as my wife sat at the counter staring at me. She felt like she had to walk on eggshells around me. It made her cringe every time she wanted to talk about changing things up.

My fight with my wife is an example of the painter not taking accountability for their painting. This was all about me. It was about my self-worth issues and feeling like a victim. I felt unworthy and like I was being taken advantage of. This made me mad, and I took it out on my wife. Bless her for sticking with me through those years. It must have been difficult. I was completely unwilling to compromise and see her side because of my own issues. This is how an unconscious creator creates.

You will come to realize that your emotions are important. You will understand that an emotionally charged reaction, such as what I experienced with my wife, is a major red flag. It is a sign for you, as the creator, to understand yourself. It is an opportunity to inquire about your beliefs. I believed I was a victim, therefore I identified myself as a victim. I behaved like I was a victim. I thought like one, I acted like one, and behaved like one. I was a creator painting art about being a victim. It was not until I realized that I was the creator with the paint brush in my hand that things shifted. I began to take accountability for my life and take accountability for my energy. The creator mindset allowed me to discover the unconscious traumas about my self-worth and self-love issues. Issues that caused me to lash out in anger over relatively simple things.

We have been indoctrinated to believe we are not powerful, and we are less than. I stated before, I am not here to ridicule anyone's religious beliefs. I am attempting to open your awareness to a different perspective. You are more powerful than you can ever imagine. You are like a child that is unaware of their own strength and power. A child that does not understand their true identity. There is so much power coursing through you, but you are being falsely led about it. You believe that you are weak and powerless. You believe there is no relationship between you and Source. It is time to change this. It is time to open to the power of Source within you and become a creator.

It is through you that Source is working its will and desire to know itself. Without Source you would not exist, nor would anything exist. You are here because of Source. You are becoming aware of the awe-inspiring power within you. It was given to you without any condition but to know yourself. You are a powerful creator, but that is because Source creates through you.

Below are some powerful and fun examples of how powerful you are.

## The New Vehicle:

Have you ever wanted to buy a vehicle? What happens when you begin that process? You think about the type you want. Will it be sedan, a truck, or a sport utility vehicle? What color do you want? Black, white, blue, red, etc. At some point you come to the vehicle you want. Let us say it is a red sedan of a particular brand. What happens next, as you move through your reality, is you become increasingly aware of the number of red sedans of the same brand on the road. It is not a coincidence. It was brought into your reality through your direct intention as the creator. You as the creator began to manifest realities that incorporate that specific red car, and it shows up everywhere.

Try it out. Pretend that you are buying a new car. Go through the process and keep an awareness out as you go about your day.

## Orange Socks:

This is a fun exercise. I want you to think about orange socks throughout the day. Truly imagine them and what they look like. Then keep an open awareness for orange socks. The likelihood is that you will project orange socks into your reality. If they do show up, it is not a coincidence. It is you as the creator manifesting oranges socks into your reality.

## The Placebo Effect:

We all have heard about the placebo effect or the sugar pill effect. When it comes to drug clinical trials, the researchers must have a control group to compare the drugs against. One half of the test subjects are given the actual medical prescription and the other half are given a sugar pill. It is common in the sugar pill control group that seventy or higher percent of the test subjects show improvement after taking the sugar pill. They have positive results of improved health even though it was just a sugar pill. This is not nonsense. This is a window into how powerful you are.

The placebo effect is direct evidence that you have more power than you are led to believe about yourself. It shows that you can heal yourself just by the way you think or what your beliefs are. How amazing is that?! You may be able to avoid medical intervention just by changing your beliefs. You have the power to heal yourself! It is an amazing idea to contemplate.

Expand the placebo effect a little further beyond just a medical trial. The placebo effect works in other areas of your life. People use the placebo effect to help them overcome obstacles in their lives. Why do you think hypnotherapy works? You get hypnotized into a false belief that would help you overcome something or become something you desire. People stop smoking or find ways to improve their health, finances, and relationships through hypnotherapy. All because of the placebo effect people's lives can change. People are creating positive change for themselves and having success creating realities that align with what they want. One's thoughts and beliefs, even though they may not be true, are becoming their reality.

This of course can go the other way as well. Believing in something that is not true about yourself can have an enormous impact. There is a vast number of people who do not reach their full potential because they believe they are not good enough. Numerous people think lesser of themselves and never accomplish their dreams because they believe something that is not true about themselves. Their fear about themselves limits them. People create disempowered realities all because they believe in an illusion. They believe in a lie.

In a very simplistic way, I am just scratching at the immense power lying dormant within you. You are a powerful being. It is time to see that about yourself. All the examples above are little insights into that power. The placebo effect is just a window into the world of becoming the creator and how powerful you can be.

There are numerous examples of humanity expanding their beliefs to accomplish things that started out as just an idea. We can create amazing things and accomplish amazing feats when we put our hearts and minds to it. Think about how many amazing things have been created through the accomplishments of the human being. Think of the great advancements we have made. Think about all the things that are created from us being human, both good and bad. We create music and art in a myriad of ways. Making instruments and finding different ways to put musical notes together. Artists expressing their energy in all sorts of ways. We dance, we sing, we play, and we are always doing something to express our energy. We are building and constructing things all the time—skyscrapers, bridges, dams, roads, airplanes, boats, etc. Humanity is always making and creating something through our own power. We are always creating, and we do not see the power of that. What other being on this planet does these things? What other being is creating things for the sheer joy of creating? We have such creative power within us, and it is taken for granted because we are taught that we are not powerful. With a different perspective you can see all the amazing things that we do. You get a sense that there is a creative force coursing through us. It is there within us because we are Source. We create because we are Source. Creating helps us understand what we are.

You are a creator and creating is a natural byproduct of your existence. Even when you are trying not to do anything you are still creating something. A creator is always creating. Whether you like it or not, you are always creating. Think about that. You are creating even though you may feel like you are doing nothing. You are creating each moment in your life and that does not necessarily mean you have to build something physically. Creation can be experiences as well.

In some instances, you may feel like you want to literally do nothing and lay down on the couch. In one perspective that might be nothing but being lazy, but in the end, you are creating an experience of doing nothing and being lazy. Nothing is a creation because nothing is something within Source. Nothing is something to experience to understand more about yourself as Source.

You are a powerful creator, but you have been completely unconscious of it. You are asleep to this knowledge, and it is time to wake up to it. It is time to stop sleeping through life. It is time to become the creator and consciously create your life.

# CHAPTER 2:
# THE LAW OF ATTRACTION

There are two main ways to describe a glass that is half filled with water. The glass is either half full or half empty. Are you a half empty or half full person? This is a simple insightful exercise for understanding how someone sees the world. Albeit simple, it is a fairly accurate indication about one's life. It is more probable than not that the person who thinks of the glass as half full is far more positive than the glass half empty person. The glass half full person is likely surrounded by more positive people and has more positive experiences in their life. In addition, they are probably happier in their marriage, relationships, and career. Lastly, the glass half full people are likely to be more opportunistic and be more financially abundant than their half empty counterparts.

This is by no accident. Positive people tend to have more success than those that are negative about life. A positive person experiences a different set of conditions or a different reality than those who see life negatively. It is by design and by intention that causes their realities to be different from each other, whether they are conscious of it or not. Like attracts like and this can be seen everywhere in our lives. Things that are vibrationally in line with each other will come together.

Working in the business and financial world, you try to find people who are more successful than you. Why is that? Because successful businesspeople have traits that make them successful. People try to mimic successful people in the hopes it may help them become more successful. When you surround yourself with successful people you learn about their behaviors, their habits, and their beliefs. You begin to adopt these traits and energies as your own. It is helping you match your vibration to the same vibration or successful experiences that other successful people have. You become a match to the energy by becoming their energy.

That is why so many people try to emulate incredibly successful people. In the financial industry, people like Warren Buffett are highly mimicked. People want the level of success he has and therefore they try to replicate his energy. They mimic his decision making by reading his books or paying for a lunch to talk to him. People will match to others based on their intentions.

What if you did the opposite and surrounded yourself with people who were unmotivated and lazy? Do you think you would attract more success and financial abundance? The likelihood is you would become unmotivated. You would become lazy and not do anything. You would miss out on all the opportunities to find success. You would vibrationally become less of a match to successful experiences.

The point I am trying to get across is that life does not happen by coincidence. Your life is not by accident. That which is your environment, your friends and social groups surrounding you, your work, and other worldly life experiences are not by accident. They are by intention. They are the result of you working with the Universe to bend and shift to your intention. They are signaling to the Universe this is what I am, find me the same. Like attracts like.

It is not by coincidence that you are where you are in life. It is by design that you are matched to experiences based on how you think, believe, and act. The sum of your energy is like a magnet and somehow you are getting matched to things just like you. The Universe is matching your intention and energy with like energy. This is happening all the time on an energetic level. You are only aware of the physical experience of the law of attraction.

It is my belief that the energy comes first, before the physical experience of it. Everything starts with the energy and then you see the physical. When you are experiencing a physical expression, you are experiencing the lagging effect of energy.

This can be seen when it comes to you. Before you take any physical action, you had a thought. The thought moved through you, and you decided to act on that thought. The physical action of doing something came after the thought. This can be said about anything that was created in our reality. A thought becomes an idea that inspires and motivates an individual who takes the physical action steps to manifest it. Businesses came about because someone had a thought in their garage that led to an idea. That idea manifested in the physical action of doing something and creating. Thus began many companies that we know of today.

This book was an idea that inspired me into action. It started out energetically and led me to write it. It is the physical result of the energy within me. I manifested it through the physical action of doing. The physical is the result of the higher energetics manifesting in our reality. It is the lagging results of energy. The energy comes first then the physical. Take care to keep your awareness on the non-physical. It is likely the reason for why you are having your physical experience. Even physical experiences are still energy.

What we perceive as physical things in our reality are just energies in difference states of vibrations. The same Source energy that makes us is but energy of light and sound. It is separated or differentiated by the speed that it vibrates. Think about the different states the elements can be in, like water. Water can exist in three different states based on its energetic vibration. It can be in a solid state when cooled. As the energetic vibration of the water molecules almost come to a standstill, it becomes ice. It can be in a liquid form as water molecules have more energy to move around and move up in temperature. Lastly, it can exist as a gaseous state if the energy vibration is too high to be in liquid state. Just like water, your experience of physical objects is the observation of energy vibrating at a certain rate, holding a vibrational pattern that gives it the illusion of being solid. Physical objects are just energies of light and sound in difference states of vibration. We exert our conscious on these energies and affect our reality.

We are fully participating in our lives as creators. We are constantly creating our reality based on forces we exert onto it. We affect the arrangement of light and sound by our consciousness. The world or reality which we exist in is shifting to match our consciousness. As you walk around there is a force being exerted by you. It is a vibration or a frequency that rings out into the world. This vibrational force of thoughts, beliefs, and actions magnetizes energies that are in alignment with your energy. Anything that is not a magnetic match gets repelled. The Universe is constantly bringing vibrational matches to you like a magnet. This is what we call the law of attraction.

Imagine if you will, a soup of energy that is life force that is all around you. The science community calls this the quantum field. In the spiritual world, it may be called *prana*. This field reacts to consciousness. It comes alive when consciousness flows through with intent and creates a magnetic pull. The stronger the flow of life force the stronger the magnetic pull. The energetic field of light and sound will arrange itself to that intention in the most efficient manner. The law of attraction is just that. It is Source energy of light and sound being attracted to you because of your vibration. It is drawn to you like a magnetic pull.

You may have read some materials on the law of attraction, or you may have watched a video on it. Much of the information on this topic is about manifesting material experiences into your life. It usually revolves around materialistic things such as a new car, new house, a new relationship, new job, etc. As much as I believe that you can manifest material experiences into your life, I would rather focus on how the law of attraction is being used. The narrow focus of using the law of attraction to attain riches and material wealth feels twisted to me. It is being twisted to keep you distracted on the external rather than trying to fundamentally understand yourself. I prefer to see it as a tool to help you become aware of yourself. A mechanism for you to find more peace and happiness in your life no matter what form it comes in.

When you become of the creator mindset, you step into a state of being. It is a state that knows you are creating your life at any given moment. You become aware of the energy and your vibration that the Universe is corresponding with. There is awareness of how your reality is a projection of all the energy you hold within yourself. It is a projection from the sum of your thoughts, beliefs, and actions. The law of attraction is how the Universe delivers your reality. It is your vibration that determines what the law of attraction and the Universe bring to you. What you see around you is just the energy matching to your total energetic vibrational output or your energy field. It is like you are creating a living movie through your energy field.

Your life is like a hologram. It is a hologram in the sense that you are the projector and what you are seeing is coming from you. You are the one interpreting the world through your energy field. You are projecting your beliefs into reality and the Universe is helping you act it out. What you experience in every moment is the Universe giving you feedback on your current vibrational status. It starts with your thoughts. Those thoughts have a vibration, and the consistent state of those thoughts generate your frequency. Those thoughts, if consistent enough, become a belief. A belief is an energetic pattern setup that sends out a frequency into the Universe. The Universe responds and sends you energetic vibrations that are an exact match. The Universe is reflecting your frequency by sending you things, events, people, etc., that align or are a match to your vibration. You will experience things that are an exact vibrational match to what you are vibrating at.

What we are told and is reinforced in our life is that the physical is the only thing that is real. We focus on the physical because our senses tell us what to believe. Seeing is believing. We believe what we can see, smell, touch, hear, and taste. It must be tangible for us to accept it as part of our beliefs. Again, those beliefs keep you limited and there are far more energies and realities at play. There is far more than what we can discern with our physical five senses.

For instance, our physical eyes can only see the visible light spectrum. See Figure 1[1]. The visible light spectrum is a fraction of the known range of frequencies that exist. Our eyes can only interpret a sliver of what is there. There are far more energies beyond the visible light spectrum than what we can see. What you interpret as your reality through your eyes is not the whole truth. You are only getting a fraction of it. There are also gamma rays, x-rays, microwaves, ultraviolet, cosmic, and infrared to name a few that you cannot see. There exists far more to your reality than what you can physically see. Just because you cannot see it, smell it, taste it, feel it, or hear it does not mean it does not exist. Think of the potential of what you could be missing just because you are focused on your physical sight. Much like your sight, there are decibels in hertz that are lower or higher than your audible ability. Dogs hear far more than you or I. Radio waves are flying around unbeknownst to us, but because we have technology such as antennas on a radio, we can hear

---

1    Quora(website); "What percentage of the light spectrum are humans able to see with their eyes?," updated July 22, 2019, https://www.quora.com/What-percentage-of-the-light-spectrum-are-humans-able-to-see-with-their-eyes

what is being broadcast. This applies to all your senses. There is more to your reality than what you are experiencing through your five senses. Just because you cannot perceive it, does not mean it is not real. Open your perspective that there is more at play here than just the physical.

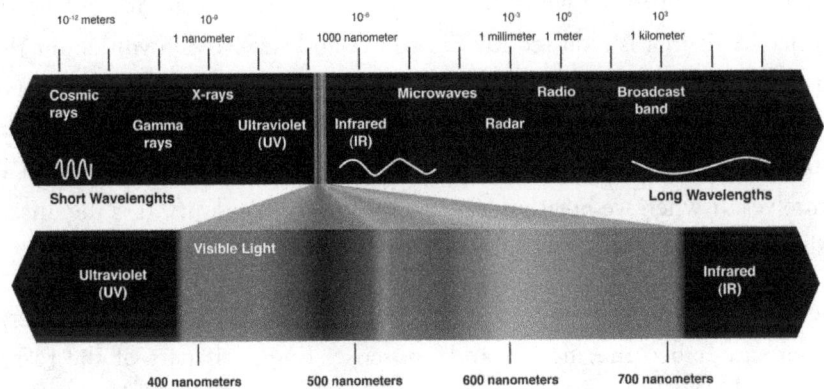

In fact, what you are interpreting with your five senses is merely a translation of your mind. You take in the physical sensations, the physical stimuli sent through your physical body via the nervous system, and your mind translates the electrical information into something you can interpret. The stimuli that you receive is interpreted through the filters and experiences into electronic information to fit into your belief system. Everything is happening in your head. That is why I say that your life is like a hologram. You are projecting a hologram of your reality in your head. You are the one projecting the information you are sensing with your five senses. You are creating a reality that is based on limited beliefs of just the physical.

What I am trying to get you to understand or what I am trying to emphasize to you is that there is far more than the physical at play here. Energy is just as important and it is everywhere. It is beyond what you can sense but it is directly affecting your reality. You cannot rely solely on the physical. It is the intangible things, the unseen forces, the thoughts, ideas, and beliefs that have far more impact on your reality than the slow and lagging physical action that we are told.

Every day we experience the element of air in our lives. You cannot see the air that we breathe, but you accept that it is there. You accept that it is real and part of your reality. Why? Perhaps it is because we can see the effects of that air. You see the lagging effect of the air as it moves through your environment. You observe trees swaying and leaves blowing in the wind. You can feel it on your skin as it moves around you. It is the air being focused and placed under pressure that creates the winds and the physical results of it. You inhale the oxygenated air that is required for you to live and survive. Do you doubt that air is real? Do you doubt that the air exists because you cannot see it? No. Many of us do not question the reason or think that the trees are swaying on their own. We do not doubt it when we see leaves swirling around by themselves or when we breathe out steam when it is cold out. It is the unseen air that we attribute that to.

When it comes to our physical lives, we completely disregard the energy component. It becomes fiction and nonsense. Energy is part of the reason why something happens, but we do not see it that way. We think we are just dealing with only the physical. The cause and effect are not just physical with our reality. Why do you observe the physical effects of your reality and doubt there are underlying energetic or unseen forces at play? There are real forces at play. There is real energy at work here. It is undeniable that there are unseen forces that impact our everyday lives. Energy comes first then the physical. Open your perspective to that there is more than just what your physical senses can pick up.

## ENERGY AND VIBRATION:

You are a divine Source being. You are an energetic being. Source energy runs through you and what you think and feel gives off a vibration. Vibrations of sound and light. You are a conscious being of Source and of sound and light that moves around. It is hard to tell, but you have an energy field around you. It is magnetic and it is charged just like a battery. It is hard to see, but like above, regarding the light spectrum, there is more than meets your physical senses.

Much like the visible light spectrum, there is spectrum of vibrational output that you are giving out. Let us continue with the light spectrum metaphor to maintain consistency. Each color on the light spectrum is located at a certain wavelength or vibration. Red would be the slowest wavelength and the violet would be the fastest. Everything else in between is associated with its own wavelength that falls between red and violet. The rate at which something vibrates does not denote a level of importance but rather to indicate there is a rate of speed difference. At different vibrational speeds or rates, one would have an entirely different experience in colors. With a slight change in vibration in the light spectrum, you are jumping from one color to a completely different color. The experience of one color would be a vastly different experience from another color. You would experience two completely different realities.

Much like yourself, your vibrational state of being can have immense differences. Your experience of one set of vibrations could be vastly different from the next. Your feelings are much the same way. Your emotions have different vibrational locales. Those differences in vibrations can generate worlds of differences in your emotions. The vibration of sadness feels far different than the feeling of happy. In a linear sense, you can say that sadness feels lower and slower in vibration compared to feeling happy which is higher and faster in vibration. The experience of sadness reflects a world much different than when you are experiencing happiness. Have you ever seen someone who is happy standing next to someone who is sad? They are completely two different people, and they see the world completely differently as well. Their realities are different vibrationally.

These energetic vibrations called your emotions exist within you all at the same time. You do not have to go anywhere, you do not have travel, nor do you have to change your external environment to experience them. Within your singular space, you can experience many different vibrations just through feeling your emotions or your emotions state. Your emotions are key to understand the law of attraction.

The law of attraction is the magnetic attraction in your reality based on what you are focusing on or putting your intention into. What you are putting your focus on will manifest or attract into your reality. My way of looking at the law of attraction is the matching of frequencies, rather than a mental focus concept. The law of attraction is in relation to far more that what you put your intention into. It is in relationship to your entire being as a vibration. It is how you, as a creator being, manifest your reality. It is how you experience things to know more about yourself.

You are taking the substance that is life and creating a current or flow by your vibrational intention. That current or flow becomes magnetic when enough life substance moves through you. If it is a strong enough force of magnetic energy, then it will draw other like frequencies into it. Like a magnet, you are attracting into your life things that match up with your energy or your vibration. The Universe is the matchmaker that brings you the experiences that are a match to you.

The Universe likes to match up frequencies. It does not care what you like and desire, it cares about what your frequency is. It cares about the magnet that you are carrying around. Like things attract each other. Things of opposites repel each other. The issue is that many of us are maneuvering through our day completely unaware of the magnetic force we are exerting. You run around unconscious of your magnetic pull, and you pick up things that are going to weigh you down. Many of us have no clue about our vibration and what it does to us and our reality. So, we need to understand what the Universe is looking to match. The best way to think of this is to look at two different emotions: happy and sad.

Try to remember the last time you felt happy. What did it feel like in your body? How did it feel energetically? You likely felt lighter in the body, you felt more energetic, and you had a positive outlook. Things are more fun, brighter, and easier. The energy for feeling happy has a vibrational signature or frequency. The same goes for feeling sad. Recall the last time you were sad. How did that feel in your body? How did you feel energetically? Mentally? There is a vast difference between the two emotions and each have their own frequency. It is almost like you are in two different worlds.

The vibration of happiness is a completely different world compared to feeling sad. For each moment you are holding on to the frequency of happiness the Universe will help create or magnetize to you, via the law of attraction, the same vibrational match to happiness. The same goes for sadness. If you hold on to sadness and create your moments with sadness, then you will magnetize from the Universe vibrational matches of sadness. In a hierarchical sense, you can say that feeling happy is a higher vibration than feeling sad. This gives insight into the concepts of vibrations and what the law of attraction is based on.

Let us take the explanation of the two figures from before and how that works. The happy figure thinks positively. The consistent thoughts of being positive generate a frequency. That positive frequency is emitted out into the Universe. The Universe receives the frequency and responds to the call. The Universe sends back energy that is a vibrational match to the positive frequency being emitted. The positive figure receives the Universal input and interprets the energy as positive feedback. Thus, supporting the positive person's thought process and reinforcing their belief.

Now, let us take the not happy figure. The not happy figure thinks negatively. The consistent thoughts of being negative generate a frequency. That negative frequency is emitted out into the Universe. The Universe receives the frequency and responds to the call. The Universe sends back energy that is a vibrational match to the negative frequency being emitted. The negative figure receives the Universal input and interprets the energy as negative feedback. Thus, supporting their thought process and reinforcing their belief.

That is an overly simplistic example, but hopefully you get the understanding. Let us take this a step further. Consider a person who thinks negatively about themself, and we will call this person Sam. Sam is holding the energetic vibration of feeling "not worthy." Each morning Sam gets up and goes to work. The first thought that Sam has in the morning is, *I can't believe I have to go to work today at this crummy job.* He gets out of bed and heads to the bathroom. Sam looks in the mirror and says, *My gosh, I look like crap. Look at my hair, look at me, I am balding. No one wants to date a balding man. Oh, man, I am so fat! Look at my belly!* After his morning routine, he goes downstairs and eats some cereal for breakfast. Sam accidentally spills the bowl of cereal and it goes everywhere. *I am such a clumsy idiot!* He cleans up and heads to work. No one says "hi" to him and he just sits at his desk. *This day is going to drag, and I hope I don't get bothered.* Not more than a few minutes later, Sam is interrupted by his boss who points out a mistake he made. Sam thinks to himself after the encounter, *I cannot believe I did that! I hope I don't lose my job!*

Someone who holds a different vibration and energy of positive thinking would experience a completely different reality. To compare a positive thought pattern against the example above is truly not viable because that person's reality would not be the same. They would have a different job, different friends, different looks, etc. The reason behind this is because of the law of attraction. If one were to hold on to the "worthy" versus "not worthy" their reality would be drawn to completely different experiences. They would be magnetized to experiences that would make them feel worthy. Someone who feels unworthy would be drawn to experiences to reinforce their unworthiness.

To play along, let us take the same example. Sam is holding the energetic vibration of feeling "worthy." Each morning Sam gets up and goes to work. The first thought that Sam has in the morning is, *Oh it's a new day and I look forward to seeing my work friends.* He jumps out of bed and heads to the bathroom. Sam looks in the mirror and says, *My gosh, I feel good. Look at my hair. Look at me, I am balding. But I am okay with that.* After his morning routine, he goes downstairs and has cereal for breakfast. Sam accidentally spills the bowl of cereal and it goes everywhere. *Whoops, glad that wasn't a huge mess!* He cleans up and heads to work. Sam notices someone saying "good morning" to him as he commutes to work and starts a conversation. *I am going to be productive today.* Not more than a few minutes later, Sam is interrupted by his boss who points out how good his work has been. Sam thinks to himself after the encounter, *I think I am going to get a promotion.*

Have you ever wondered why people who tend to be happier are typically healthier? They spend more time outside, they eat better, and they treat themselves better. They are upbeat and probably less stressed. This affects the physical body and overall attitude. If you compare that person to someone who is always sick, you will likely find them to be more stressed. Their diet is likely not the best and they are physically out of shape. Like attracts like. Your vibration is dictating this.

Take an example of people on a plane. Why is it that some people get sick, and some do not? You are enclosed in an airtight vehicle, breathing in the same air for hours, and subject to the same cold, virus, bacterium, or sickness variants flying around. By medical and scientific reasoning, everyone should get sick, but not everyone does. Yes, of course, some peoples' immune systems are better able to fight it off. That is an indication some people are in better health and have a stronger immune system. This means they are vibrating at a much different rate than what the illness or sickness is vibrating at. These people are generally less likely to get sick compared to the immune compromised people who are stressed out and think lowly about themselves. From my perspective, it is because some people on that plane are an exact vibrational match to that sickness and some are not. It is your overall vibration that plays a role in whether you get sick or not.

It is your thoughts and beliefs that instruct the law of attraction. It is imperative you try to understand how you think because it is affecting it. The way you think about yourself from how your day goes to how your body looks and more is constantly talking to the Universe. If your frequency is about self-worth and not feeling worthy, you will draw into your personal hologram infinite experiences that make you feel unworthy. The law of attraction will show it everywhere, from jobs, friends, financial, health, etc. It will surround you with what you believe to be true.

Before you took any action in your life, you had a thought. It became an idea that sprung from the well within you to be a desire. With inspiration and willpower you took physical steps towards attaining your desire. Action is but the energy in motion after the energy foundation was set up. The physical comes because of the law of attraction. The higher vibrational energy of thoughts and beliefs is in relationship to the law of attraction. It must not be discounted.

## THE UNIVERSE

The Universe is a beneficial energy. It is UNCONDITIONAL love. What does unconditional mean? You are loved without conditions. It is given freely without any expectations back. It does not care if you are good or bad. It does not hold back things because you did not play nice. It only cares that you are made of the same energy and consciousness as it is, and it will support your expansion by any means necessary. No expense spared. It does so because you and the Universe are part of the same thing.

Remember that you are Source seeking to understand itself. The Universe wants to show you what you want because it too seeks to understand itself. It wants to come alive and expand on your beliefs in all the myriads that creations may have because it desires to know itself. The Universe will explode to life with whatever you put your intention or focus on. It will explode to life because the Universe and Source want to see it and experience it. Source wants to be found; Source wants to know itself. Whatever you put your thoughts into, the Universe will bring to you whatever you need to fully expand on that expression of energy.

Since you are the Universe and the Universe is you, it will deliver unto you all that you desire. But it only works through your energy. Energy is not linear. Energy is not human and does not speak linear human languages. Energy is beyond time and space. It does not communicate, and it does not act like the way you and I have been taught. It understands intention and vibration.

When you speak out, "I desire_____," fill in the blank. The Universe does not know what the *blank* is. It does not know the "what" to your desire. It seeks to know the energy behind the desire and match that. When you say, "I desire _____," but your energy and vibrational signature say something else, then the Universe will not expand on your desire. It will respond to what your vibrational intent is. The Universe will always deliver based on your projected intention or vibration. It will always match the level of consciousness that you are applying your intention to.

I remember a time my young daughter needed help looking for a toy. I asked her if she even looked. She replied, "Yes, I looked everywhere." Which I could clearly tell she did not. I told her to use her eyes and open them up. In which she proceeded to peel her eyes open further with her fingers and look around. I told her what I wanted her to do, except her interpretation of that was very literal. The Universe is much like a child in the sense of its literal understanding. You may be aware of what you want but how that transfers to the Universe is different.

## HOW YOU INTERACT WITH THE UNIVERSE

You are attracting into your life the exact match to the sum of your frequency. The vibrational output, whether you are conscious or unconscious of it, will be matched by the Universe. The Universe will bring to you these experiences in the most efficient and effective manner. It will work like a well-oiled machine to align you with the exact vibration match for you to know more about yourself.

The Universe does not care about form. It cares about vibration. It cares to show you what your vibration is by patterning out the same vibrational experiences into your reality. You go about your life unconsciously exerting a frequency. That frequency resonates out into the Universe and the Universe responds. It will manifest into your reality experiences that match up to your frequency. Those experiences can come in any form, shape, or way to help you confirm the frequency you are holding on to. It will confirm your beliefs.

Think about the last time you got angry. Think about all the actions and experiences that came about while you moved about in an angry state. Did you notice that things kept perpetuating the anger? Did you notice that everything you did just created more anger? I recall getting angry with my wife once as I was trying to get my daughter into the car. We were running late, and I needed my daughter to get into the car. I was looking for control and everything felt like I was not in control. In dealing with it, I got angry. In a rage, I yelled at my daughter. She then started to cry and wanted her mother. This made me even more angry which led me to yelling at my wife for being unsupportive. She began to argue back at me, and I got even more angry. This led to feeling explosive and I began punching our garage door. I made a fist dent in the door which hurt my hand. That made me ever angrier, and I decided to kick the door. My wife yelled at me even more because I damaged the door and I yelled back some explosive expletive and stormed off.

As you can see, you continue to magnetize experiences to match your energy. The Universe will continue to match and resonate with you until something changes. Imagine if you will, two tuning forks. You take one tuning fork and tap it on the table. It begins to vibrate out and hold a frequency. As you bring the tuning fork next to other tuning fork, you will notice that the second one will begin to pick up the resonance from the first. It becomes one resonance, vibrating together at the exact same frequency.

That is how you and the Universe interact with each other. You are resonating out a frequency every day and as you move around the Universe resonates with you at that same frequency. The law of attraction is what we call the magnetic force that draws in your reality. The Universe holds all the potentials for that magnetic force to work.

## DUALITY AND POLARITY

I would be absent-minded if I were not to discuss duality. There is a spiritual concept that states that for what you care to experience in your life requires you to know yourself by the opposite. Duality is the basic understanding that there is an opposite force to the force you are trying to impose. It is an instance of opposition or contrast between two concepts or two aspects of the same thing. By physics definition, it is the quantum-mechanical property of being regarded as both a wave and a particle. The latter definition applies deeply to what we are talking about. This is because the Universe, depending on perception of your intent, can be both negative and positive at the same time.

You are Source seeking to understand itself. For you to know one thing, you must experience the opposite. For example, you cannot understand being poor unless you experience being wealthy. You cannot know what it is like to be abundant if you do not know what lack is. You cannot fully understand victimhood unless you have a perpetrator. You cannot fully understand happiness unless you understand what sadness is. This is the feast and famine, life and death, light and dark, yin and yang, love and fear, black and white, etc. We come to know ourselves through experience of the opposite in varying degrees.

There is a scientific photo that shows an image of an electron. It is a photo that captures an electron being in two different places at once. How amazing is that?! How can something be in two places at once? Yet, there it is, shown by the photo. This is direct evidence that something can exist in two different places at the same time. Why is that important? Well, from a physics standpoint, this implies the quantum nature of our Universe and the implications of human consciousness on matter. But for this body of text, it implies that which we perceive can be both here and there. It can be neither and either, or it can be good and bad. The point being that what you perceive is only a matter of truth to the observer.

The electron being in two different places indicates that it can be in one place or both. It depends on the creator observing it. The Universe stands in a suspended state until the law of attraction is brought in. The Universe is quantum, being both here and there at the same time, until the creator observes it. When the creator decides to observe it, the Universe becomes what it needs to be to be seen. It can either contrast the creator's beliefs or validate the creator's beliefs. That is why light has properties that show it as a particle and show it as a wave. It can be two different things depending on the observer. The observer is the creator, and the law of attraction is being used to create polarity or duality.

The reason duality is so important regarding the law of attraction is because you, as the creator, must understand yourself through the opposite. The experiences in your life are showing only one perspective to your truth. There can exist and there does exist at same time, an opposite and opposing force. In reality, the two are not separate from each other but are whole. They are one of the same, but it is your perspective as the creator that gives it life and meaning. The law of attraction uses the polarity to validate the meaning you have given it.

Duality is intrinsic to the law of attraction. The more emotional charge you place with an intention to experience something, the same will go for the other side. I state this to help you understand that we must be mindful of the things we are trying to manifest in our lives. Especially when you are unaware of yourself and the unconscious patterns you are holding. Without undue review or circumspect understanding, you could inadvertently continue the same experience you are trying to get out of.

# CHAPTER 3:
# BEAUTY IS IN THE EYE
# OF THE CREATOR

Every day we are using our senses. You are constantly sensing the world through your five physical senses. The electrical data is sent via our nervous system into the brain. It is within the mind that we interpret the information into the world as we understand it. It is within the mind all is done. For instance, imagine we pick an apple from a tree and take a bite from it. It is within the mind we interpret the redness of the apple that we see. The taste that it brings when we bite into it. The feel of the tension and apple skin as we pluck it from the tree. The sounds it makes as we bite into the crispness of the apple. The smell of the apple as we pierce the skin. It is all being interpreted within the mind.

In fact, everything you are experiencing is a projection through the mind. You are interpreting everything that is coming through your senses. It is your mind that interprets what the world smells like, feels like, sounds like, tastes like, and looks like. Your mind is the interpreter of all the stimuli that comes through your physical senses. It interprets all the information for you to understand it.

You are essentially creating your reality by what you interpret through your physical senses. It is like you are projecting a hologram in your head based on how your mind deciphers the stimuli. Like a projector at a movie theatre, it is reading or taking in the information from the film strip and projecting it onto a screen. You are seeing reality on a screen that is being projected from within the mind. Everything is happening in your head. You are the one watching it.

Take a second and close your eyes. What happens to the outside world? It goes away. With no stimuli through your eyes, you cannot project the world in your brain. You can still interpret the world through your other senses, but the visual world disappears. Of course, you can imagine what things look like and where they are, but that is still occurring in your head.

When you open your eyes, the stimuli immediately flow into the brain and the world projects again. The world comes alive again through your vision. Let us imagine that you are color-blind. How would the world be different to you? How does that change your perspective? If your senses are being filtered, then your experience of the world could become distorted. It would be different from another person who has a "normal" perspective of the world. What if your interpretation of the world is filtered through an energy that is mostly negative energy? How would the world look? What if the world was filtered through a more positive energy? What would your interpretation of the world be then? This is how your beliefs are affecting how you are seeing the world.

Everything is energy. That energy is filtered through your energy field. You are filtering the energetic stimuli to fit your beliefs and your energy field. This is to understand it from your level of consciousness. What you are projecting outward is your interpretation of that energy filtering through your own energy system. You are essentially experiencing your own energy that is being broadcast within your mind. In some way and in some form, you are experiencing yourself through the energy that is being seen in your reality. Whatever you may witness or experience is coming from you. You are the one creating the projection through your energy field.

This is vitally important to understanding the concept of the mirror. You are the one projecting your reality through your mind. At some level, everything is happening within you. As I say, the law of attraction is based on your vibration. What you are experiencing in your reality, in some way, is in vibrational accordance with you. You are a vibrational match because it is coming through you. Not matter how far removed it may feel, it is still being interpreted through your energy field. If you are experiencing it in your reality, then there is some aspect of you that is being conveyed. This is because the energy had to be filtered through your senses. It had to be filtered through your mind. It had to be interpreted in the mind. It had to come through your entire energy field and your belief system for you to be experiencing what you are going through in your life now. You are projecting the movie that you are engaging with. It is time you questioned why you are projecting the movie you are watching. This is done through the mirror concept.

## THE MIRROR

At some point in the day, you will see yourself in a mirror. Whether that is in the morning as you get ready or on your drive to work, you at some point will look into a mirror. I usually see one when I walk into my bathroom first thing in the morning. I usually stare at myself for a brief second. I notice what I look like: my morning bedhead, slightly sleepy eyes, and wearing comfy sleeping clothes. Sometimes I comment about my looks or mumble something about how I need to get ready, or that I look tired or rested (depending on how I slept that night). After I shower and get ready, I check myself in the mirror again and see if I look okay and head out.

The mirror is a tool for me to see myself in my process from waking up to heading out the door. It allows me to check in with myself and observe myself. It allows me to see myself standing there in different states of morning routine. Do I like what I am seeing? Am I missing something? Do I need to recomb my hair, or did I forget to shave? It helps me evaluate what I am experiencing as I move around.

The concept of the mirror is much like the physical mirror I use in my bathroom. The mirror is the concept about reflection. A mirror is reflecting or mirroring back the image of you. This concept is applied to you and your reality. What you are experiencing in your reality, all of your experiences are but a mirror or a reflection of yourself. Not in a physical sense, but in an energetic sense. What you experience in your reality is a mirror of your beliefs, energy, and vibration. This mirror concept helps you see and observe yourself. Much like when I look into the mirror during my morning routine. I would not be able to see my reflection and what I look like if there was no mirror. The mirror concept is needed in order to observe yourself as the creator. It helps you extrapolate information about how you are creating your experiences. It is a tool to learn about who you are.

Now that you understand how to step into your power by being the creator and you understand the law of attraction, you can understand the mirror. The mirror is how you as a creator get to understand yourself and what you are creating. This is the first step to healing and empowering yourself.

There is a phrase that is frequently thrown around in the spiritual community that is credited to Hermes Trismegistus. The phrase is, "As above so below, as within so without." This is an important phrase. What is being stated here on a linearity perspective is that what is above you will be reflected below and vice versa. It is also stating that what is within you will also be on the outside. This is because you are Source expanding itself upon itself. All that you see in existence is Source seeing itself within itself. You are experiencing yourself through the reality of which you exist in as a projection from you. What you see in the external world must exist inside you. For if it did not, then it would not show up. Therefore, what you are seeing is a giant mirror to help you understand yourself as Source. The external world is an exact reflection of what is within you, for if it did not exist within you, it would not be seen externally. As above so below, as within so without.

Everything has purpose and can be used as a mirror. This is because it all came through you and reflects the self. That means even the smallest pebble has a purpose. It is there because you made it so. It came to be because you projected it through your energy. It has a reason to be there and can provide meaning, should you decide to give it meaning. It can be used as a mirror to understand yourself.

As you go about your day, try to see the world as a creator. At every moment, whether you like it or not, or whether you know it or not, you are creating or co-creating your reality. The vibratory reality that you see is based on your energy. It encompasses the vibrational sum of all your thoughts, beliefs, and actions. What you see in your reality is like a hologram of your inner workings. As you are projecting your reality, all the energy that you hold within yourself is being filtered into your reality. You must become aware that everything you see is merely a reflection of what you are holding on to. The Universe brings to you, via the law of attraction, the experiences you need to see what your thoughts and beliefs are. Therefore, the tiniest pebble to the grandness of the Universe is but an opportunity to see something about yourself. It is in every moment of your reality that something energetically is being reflected back to you about what you are. It can only be done if you can see into the mirror.

As a creator, you require the law of attraction to experience what you are creating. It allows you to experience your thoughts, beliefs, and actions aligning with you. How else are you to know what you are doing? Experience is needed to learn. The law of attraction is how you receive feedback from the Universe. It is for you to experience yourself. The law of attraction uses the energy and the beliefs within you. Via the law of attraction, you experience your energy. Through the tool of the mirror, you get to understand yourself and decide how to respond to it. Do you like it? No. What was reflected back to you in the mirror that occurred through the experience? What beliefs were reflected back through your experience? This is how you empower yourself as the creator. The mirror shows you what to change if you can see the mirror in the experience. The mirror and the reflections that you receive, via the law of attraction, are how you understand yourself as Source. It is how you understand you.

We mentioned in Chapter 2 that the concern for a majority of people around the law of attraction is creating materialism. They try to harness it as a tool. The law of attraction is not a tool. It is just how things work. It is a law. The mirror is the tool that is needed. When people try to use the law of attraction as a tool to manifest a materialistic experience, they miss what the law of attraction is working from. They miss the mirror to see what, why, or how things are the way they are now. They never investigate into the mirror to understand why they desire to manifest these materialistic experiences, nor do they understand why they are creating their reality that they wish so desperately to change. If they did investigate into the mirror, they may find the mirror reflects back to them a deep seeded trauma that they are trying to avoid. The creator requires the mirror to understand themselves. It requires the mirror to see the unconscious beliefs you may have. That depends on how willing the creator is to investigate themselves because of the mirror. A mirror will only reflect as far as the creator will go.

Most of my life was based in a victimhood mentality. Given my early childhood, I carried this belief that I was a victim. Things that happened to me were filtered with a victimhood mentality and I was seeing life through a victimhood lens. I would interpret much of my life as victim-based experiences. Like when I got an injury playing sports, needed to spend money to fix things, dealing with issues at work, or some business not getting my order right. You name it, I felt like a victim in some way if things did not go my way. This mentality affected my work as well.

I remember when a client decided to leave the financial planning firm I was with. I was responsible for the client relationship. After some time with us, they expressed that I did not communicate enough and decided to go a different route. It came as a shock to me. I felt that our relationship was great and that I provided sound financial advice. They had expressed their satisfaction when we talked, but it was too few and far in between to their liking. I felt like a victim. I worried about what to say to my boss. I started to worry about all my other relationships. I started to second guess my ability as an advisor.

It took the mirror for me to understand the experience. The mirror showed me what I was holding on to. It helped me understand my self-worth issues and the victimhood mentality. Without the mirror you cannot see yourself in the experience. You cannot take accountability for your actions. You cannot understand yourself. To understand yourself you must see that you were part of the creation.

We all have some kind of lens on us. It is part of being human. Most of those lenses are limiting and fear based. If I did not examine that experience that I had with my client, I would have completely missed the mirror being shown to me. I would have missed the opportunity to discover the unconscious lens that I was wearing, coloring my world view. To start to examine our lenses requires the awareness of the mirror in the experience. It takes your accountability for what happens as the creator and to see your reflection from the experience.

## CO-CREATION

Have you tried to play a multi-player game by yourself? Not much fun, is it? Try playing a board game by yourself. It is hard to get a sense of the game when it is by yourself. It's definitely not as fun when you are switching places, constantly pretending to be other players on the board. You take your turn then pretend to be another player and take a turn, etc. You do not get as excited by it. Being all of the players makes it hard to feel like you are winning or losing in the game. This is why we need others to play with.

The game is far better when you have other people playing. You do not know what they are thinking, you are uncertain about what they will do, and you have far more fun. You get to observe their movements and what how they react as you compete to win. It is a social interaction that provides lots of excitement between you and the other players.

Playing a board game with other players is akin to our lives. It brings the same enjoyment and learning experience we have with board games but in a much grander scale when we have other people involved. Family, friends, co-workers, strangers, and even enemies all offer us the diversity of excitement and learning experiences we desire. Of course, we can learn something about ourselves by playing alone, but the truth is we learn a lot more with others.

Remember that you are Source seeking to understand yourself as Source. As a spark of Source, you are creating and experiencing with other Source beings to learn more. You move around reality experiencing yourself through the veil of your temporary identity. It makes the experiences more real and the lessons far deeper.

This is what we call a co-created experience. It is when another creator creates an experience with you. It is all for the sake of understanding yourselves in this grand experiment from Source. The co-created event comes together as each creator desires to manifest an expression of themselves. This leads us to have many different experiences in our lives. The idea is for you to see a deeper mirror or reflection of self.

Your experience with another is an opportunity to peer deep within. Other co-creators are magnetized into your experience to expand or reflect the beliefs that you are holding on to. When you place an intention or put your consciousness into something, the Universe wants to see it. It comes alive to help you understand the energy. In more cases than not, this involves other creators to help co-create the lesson or experience.

Co-created experiences are gateways for you to understand yourself. Do not miss the opportunity that a co-created experience can offer. You play a role for the other co-creator and vice versa. Each are playing specific roles that we are seeking to understand about ourselves. It is through the co-creation we learn about polarity or duality. You learn about what you do not resonate with. You learn about the opposite of your belief system.

Your belief system or patterns in your life need to be perpetuated and reinforced. We need things to help us understand our intention. Polarity is part of that process. Polarity helps us see deeper into the mirror of who we are. How would you know about yourself without something to compare yourself to? Much of our experiences are about showing us what we are not so that we can get a sense of what we are. The Universe wants to show you through any means to help you understand your beliefs. That comes with understanding the opposite.

We come to know ourselves through the opposite. The polarity of our creations helps us understand our beliefs and our world is full of polarities. There is north and south, east and west, hot and cold, rich and poor, feast and famine, and dark and light. There are many polar opposites for the creators to observe. How can the soul know what it is like be to a victim if there is no perpetrator? How can one feel betrayed if there is no one to betray you? How can there be good without someone showing you what bad is? How can you understand abandonment without someone to abandon you? How can you know loss without something to lose? How can you know love without someone to love? These roles that co-creators play for us in many ways are direct opposition to our energy. Co-creators are beautiful mirrors for us, especially when they play opposing roles for us.

We need co-creators to help us play these roles for us. To help us fully understand the depth of our emotions and the connections associated with them. It is part of the components which Source desires to understand itself. We are meant to understand ourselves through co-creations. Do not underestimate the relationship that co-creators play for us. It is through love that they create these experiences, even when it does not feel that way. It is love that helps you see more about yourself, and we must honor the co-creator relationship.

# RELATIONSHIPS

In this day and age, with the advancement of technology, we are less inclined to have personal face-to-face interactions. We are far more distant from each other than ever before, even though technology has eliminated distance. This tends to lead us to more superficial relationships or ones that are fairly shallow.

I cannot emphasize how important relationships are to you as the creator. Whether romantic or not, it is hard to see something about yourself when you are alone. As mentioned above with co-creators, it is much easier and far more powerful when you have someone to play a role with you. That being said, close relationships are powerful and wonderful mirrors. The stronger and closer the relationship the better the mirror.

As a parent, children can be a great mirror. Most parents can agree here. They are constantly reflecting my control issues, my anger, my safety, and unloved feelings I have within me. They will bring back your traumas as if you were seeing yourself in them as they grow older. I recall when my daughter turned four. It was like looking into the past. The experiences with her made it a difficult year because so much trauma was being mirrored back to me. I was seeing myself all over again. The hardest part was seeing my father through me as I reacted to all the triggering events.

I remember yelling at her once because she would not listen to me. I picked her up and put her into a room. I remember holding the door and yelling, "You don't get to come out until you calm down and listen!" She was screaming and crying and trying to yank the door to open. I was feeling this terrible feeling in my body. It was at that moment I relived the memories of my father locking me in a room and not allowing to come out. Control, safety, victimhood, and self-love . . . all of it was coming back to me through my experience with my daughter. That was the mirror reflecting everything I had within me.

Honor your relationships. They are important. If you don't have children and you are married, it is typically your spouse or partner. If you are not married, it is your significant other. No romantic relationship then family. No family then your friends and co-workers. Whomever you have your deepest relationship with is your best mirror. The reason is because of trust and vulnerability. A relationship that can develop to a point where you can let your guard down and be yourself around someone, then you have a great mirror. The biggest arguments are likely with the ones who are closest to you. This is because you are accepting them to be part of you to such a degree that you feel deeply connected. There is a likelihood that you share the same energetic issues as they do. You match frequency and since you allowed them to energetically be merged with you, you see the hardest things to look at. They reflect in the experiences you have with them the things you like and dislike about yourself.

Honor those relationships because you will not find a better mirror. They are the ones who can get the closest to you and help you see the deepest things about yourself. If I have a heated argument with my spouse about something, that relationship was close enough for the hidden pieces of me to lash out. My spouse was able to energetically drag out what was hidden to be front and center through the argument.

Without deep relationships, you do not get to see deep enough. It is hard to get a deep insight with a stranger on the street. You may be able to extrapolate some information, but it would be far more difficult than one with a deeply personal relationship. Think about superficial relationships—you never truly let your guard down. In some way or another we are likely hiding behaviors, actions, or personas from them. Therefore, you do not ever feel like the relationship is important enough. It does not allow you to have the type of trust or connection that will generate the roles needed for you to feel the things you have buried on the inside. It is hard to feel the hurt and betrayal within you if you do not have someone you trust enough to play the role. You do not get a chance to heal it because you do not allow yourself. This only just perpetuates the energies into your reality, and you will get the experience from other ways. The relationships can be your greatest catalysts for change. Honor them.

My biggest arguments came from two people in my life: my brother and my wife. When I was younger, my brother made me feel so angry. He was my only blood family member and closest to me at that time. We were always getting into physical confrontations. He reflected to me the control issues that I had. He never listened to me and was always defying me. It was a difficult mirror to look into because I was seeing my father in many ways.

My wife brought out a lot of the same issues. Of course, she had her own mirror issues as well. Her insecurities drew out the anger in me and that forced me to look at my own self-worth and unloved feelings. Many of those arguments were around money. Money is a great enhancer of your beliefs. I share this in Chapter 8, but money enhances the feelings and beliefs you hold on to.

I recall a fight I had with my wife about the rugs in our house. She wanted hardwood floors upstairs after we just bought a bunch of expensive furnishings for our dining room. I was triggered immediately and yelled, "Why are you never happy?! We just bought the furniture and dining set for the dining room and now this?! You want this so badly, then you pony up! This is my money. I don't see you spending yours."

## THE COLLECTIVE

Many of us tend to think that the rest of the world is not part of who we are. We think that what is going on is something outside of us. This could not be further from the truth. We are very much a part of what happens to this planet and our human collective. The human collective experience is not separate from us but an expansion of us. It is the collective agreement of all our individual vibrations. It represents the sum of all of us.

When we expand from our little circle to that of the collective, we can see that is it just a much bigger mirror. The collective is just a giant mirror that reflects our energy back to us. As creative beings, we are individually vibrating or creating a frequency that is added to the collective agreement. It becomes part of the total vibration and consciousness that is humanity and ultimately to the planet itself. Witnessing something in the collective, such as a news headline, in your personal world is also somehow a vibrational match to you as well. It is not outside of you, it is reflective of you.

You are part of the human collective. What the human collective is experiencing is also what you are experiencing individually. Some experiences may not feel that close to home with you, but you are part of humanity. Even though what you witness may feel so far removed from you, there is some aspect being mirrored if it is showing up in your reality.

This is where your internal work is needed, especially if you are feeling emotionally charged from a collective experience. That means you hold something in resonance with it. You have become vibrationally aligned with the experience. It is thrust upon you to see what is being mirrored to resolve the energy within you. So that you may change the frequency and contribute a different frequency to the whole.

Let us say there is a massive protest occurring due to racial injustice. You witness the event on the news and the event evokes an emotional reaction in you. For this example, let's imagine that anger was your emotion. The collective experience is drawing out the anger from within you. It takes the riot for you to see there is injustice in the collective. Something must be seen to be able to change it. Since you were emotionally charged from it with anger, it is thrust upon you to understand why you feel angry. You use the mirror of the riot in the collective to heal what is feeling angry within you. What is causing you to feel this anger? When you can identify the place that it comes from, then you can shift the energy within you. This helps change the frequency in the collective.

## MISUNDERSTANDING THE MIRROR

Everything is related. The law of attraction is not the only reason why something happens. The law of attraction is merely a factor that plays into the relationship to the whole. It is part or an aspect of the truth but not the absolute. It is true that you magnetize things to your vibrational nature, but that does not necessarily mean that you deserve whatever befalls you or that you meant to create it. It just means there was something for you to know yourself by. The law of attraction is merely a tool to see something about ourselves as the creator. It helps us see something, learn something, and to choose differently if we so choose to do so. It is not a scapegoat to place blame or shame one for their actions.

For instance, someone who gets diagnosed with cancer or manifests sexual abuse into their reality does not become absolute in that they deserved it or that they wanted it. Why would anyone want to have cancer or sexual abuse? Why would anyone consciously try to create that pain? People do not go out of their way to make these things occur.

It does mean, via the law of attraction, an experience was brought into their lives for some reason or to learn something about themselves. Sometimes those reasons are far beyond our human scope of understanding. To sit and try to blame and shame oneself for actively manifesting these experiences would be counterproductive. It would be a continued mind loop of frustration and pain to try to figure out why or how you could have manifested a traumatic experience into your life. It is like keeping a wound open after the initial wound occurred. It may be best to understand that an experience was created and look to heal from it. Rather than spending all your time staring at the wound and wondering why you did that, we just need to learn from it and heal. It may be good enough to know that we had an experience that caused a trauma and imprinted something into our energetic field. Now we must seek to heal it.

The law of attraction is not meant to blame nor shame. It is to help us become aware through the experience. To learn about ourselves through the law of attraction and to understand what beliefs we may hold from that experience going forward. The answers do not always lie in the way it was done, but in the lesson from it. Using the mirror as a reflection is part of that healing process.

The mirror is the experience that you receive from your creation or co-creation. It is the reaction you receive from that experience that shows you what you are holding onto energetically. When I say that everything is a mirror, I am referring to your energetic response to the experience. I am not saying the mirror is showing who you are in every person. If you come across a homeless person with mental illness, does that mean you are a homeless mentally ill person? No. That is basically associating your divine nature, your divinity, or your identity with someone else's ego. Please do not associate yourself with someone else's ego or personality. The mirror is reflecting back your co-creation in the experience and what you personally get from that experience is the mirror. It is the energetic feedback that you receive that you need to understand yourself.

Take my co-created experience with my father for example. He was an angry drunk who physically abused me. When I investigate the mirror from that co-created experience it is not to assign myself as a drunk angry abuser. That is taking on his ego and personality which does not define me. What I am investigating is what I felt from that experience. It is the energy that I receive back that is important. I feel the anger, the pain, and the hurt of the co-created experience. That experience left me feeling unloved. This is the mirror.

Another issue with the law of attraction is that people tend to focus on manifesting materialism. It is mentally focused on the physical desires. People seek validation in the physical and tend to focus or rely on the results of the physical. It is part of our nature and what we are taught. Like I said before, everything is in relationship to the whole. The physical is merely a piece of the whole. The physically minded focus means undermining the other areas which are just as important. The mental focus on manifesting material desires could be causing you to overlook aspects of yourself. Aspects that need to be healed or beliefs that are making you want something to make you feel better. We must be mindful that we are not using the law of attraction like a tool to avoid aspects of ourselves. Like mentally manifesting money because we do not feel worthy. It is not a tool. It is just part of our reality. The law of attraction is a truth. It is part of the picture. It is part of the relationship to the whole.

## YOU GIVE OUT WHAT YOU ARE

We all have little lenses on us that limit our view. These lenses limit our perspective and consciousness so that we can experience only certain things. You can only see what those lenses allow you to see and nothing outside of it. You will act accordingly to what you know and your interaction with the world will be the same. What I mean is that your reality and how you interface with it is based on the level of consciousness that you hold. Should you hold a level of consciousness that is steeped with feeling like a victim, then your interaction with the world is such. You cannot see beyond the victim perspective because it is all that you know.

That is why you can only give out what you are. If your consciousness is holding on to pain, hurt, and anger then you will only give out the same. It will ultimately be mirrored back to you via the law of attraction. If your consciousness holds on to love and compassion, then you will give out love and compassion. There is no vibrational match to someone holding on to pain, hurt, and anger to then turn around and give out love, joy, and compassion. It cannot and will not occur because the creator cannot expand from which they do not understand. They cannot understand love and expand on love if they do not hold love. That is why hurt people hurt people. Those that have trauma in pain, will continue to expand out that vibration. They will expand out the vibration of pain unto others so that they can see their own pain.

Your reality will continue to come alive with experiences that match to the judgements you have made. It must be so. It must explode to life so that you as the creator can understand the judgements that are made. This is all to help you understand yourself and decided whether or not you want to expand from the same energy. The mirror is the key here.

How many of you have looked at someone and made a judgement against them? Perhaps it was how they dressed, what they did, or where they lived. Have you ever been judged by someone else? As pointed out, at some level you are experiencing your own energy. You are the one interpreting the energy and projecting the experience. You are the creator creating the experience and the law of attraction is helping you understand it. When you judge someone or something, what are you judging? You are placing judgment on the energy that came through your own energetic field. You are interpreting the energy through your beliefs.

When a co-creator plays a role for you, you are experiencing yourself in many ways. You are experiencing yourself via the energy of how you interpret the experience, and you are experiencing another aspect of you playing a role. At some level, you must also understand that all are divine creator beings. Co-creators are just like you, divine and Source fragments experiencing themselves as all that came from Source. If you place judgements on a co-creator, are you not then rejecting their divinity? Which is judging Source itself? Then is it appropriate to say you are ultimately judging yourself? What you judge is but a judgement unto yourself. You are projecting your fear and energies that came through your system onto another self. Therefore, what you judge is but a judgement unto yourself.

Next time you look at someone, ask yourself what do I choose to give out? Do you choose to give out love? Or fear? Do you continue to reject what you see and judge it? Ultimately, the Universe will respond back accordingly. If you hold love within you, your experiences will reflect the love in your heart. If you hold fear and judge another, then the Universe continues to bring experiences to reflect the fear you have inside yourself.

# CHAPTER 4:
# RECONNECTING WITH YOURSELF

In my financial planning career, most of my time was spent helping clients maximize their financial assets for their goals. We would help clients express their long-term goals so that we could quantify them for our projections. After we established their goals, we had to determine where they stood with those goals. This was to ensure that the client had a basis, a solid footing from which they could build their financial livelihood upon. The phrase I used was, "Build a strong foundation." You need to make sure that you have a strong foundation to build the house you want. You need a strong foundation to create from.

At this point of the journey, we must rebuild our foundation. We must recreate the walls that no longer serve the purpose for the house we want. In the spiritual healing sense, the strong foundation is your understanding of yourself. It is not what you create on the outside, but what you know about yourself on the inside.

This is done through reconnecting with yourself. Many of us are running away from ourselves. We are focused on what is outside of us rather than what is inside of us. The physical reality has distracted us from ourselves for a long time. Most people's foundations are built on the external focused beliefs. This has created a populous that is disconnected from who they are and what they are. We must stop and turn our attention to ourselves now. We must reconnect with everything that is within us.

# THE DIVINE MASCULINE AND THE DIVINE FEMININE

Within you are two divine energies. The energies are the divine masculine and divine feminine. It is vitally important to understand the two energies and how they are impacting our lives. If this is a new concept to you, try to just understand that there is an energetic balance at play and both energies have different characteristics.

The divine energies are not specific to a gender architype, although they do lend themselves to the gender roles. The divine masculine and the divine feminine energies are about creation. What I am talking about here is the energies used to create and manifest things into your reality. These are like the poles associated with a battery. There is a polar positive end and a polar negative end. The positive and negative poles are not separate from the battery but are associated differently regarding energy.

Like with positive and negative energy, we have an association to a male and a female aspect. This could also be symbolized by ancient Chinese symbol of Yin and Yang or the Sanskrit concept of Ida and Pingala.

The divine feminine energy is the energy that encompasses all the potentials. It is a state that all pathways and creative manifestation can occur from. It is the right side of the brain, the creative side. It is your intuition and feelings. When we think about the divine feminine energy, we typically associate with it the following characteristics:

- Cooperation
- Equality
- Oneness
- Emotional
- Intuitive
- Heart-centered
- Compassionate
- Open
- Being
- Stillness
- Nurture

To symbolize the divine feminine energy, consider the circle in Figure 1. The circle is all encompassing. It holds everything within it. It has all the potential within the circle.

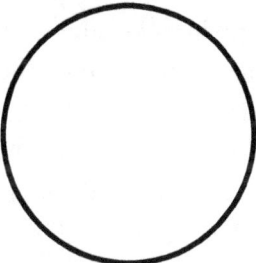

Figure 1

The divine masculine energy is energy with focused intention. It is manifesting out of the divine feminine energies to create something. It is harnessing the divine feminine energy and bringing it into manifestation. It is the left side of the brain, the logical side. It is the mind. When we think about the divine masculine energy, we typically associate the following characteristics:

- Competition
- Hierarchy
- Control
- Action
- Doing
- Results
- Logic
- Mind-centered
- Producing
- Accomplishing

To symbolize the divine masculine energy, consider the straight line in Figure 2. It is the creation of drawing a line from point A to point B. The direction and intention of movement out of singular thought.

Figure 2

So why does this matter? It matters because we are taught in an imbalanced way regarding these energies. It is important to understand these two energies so that you have an understanding of their misuses. It is important to find how we are imbalanced within so to not create with imbalanced energies.

Our society is focused on the divine masculine energies. It is wildly unbalanced toward honoring the divine masculine. Think about the history of our society. We have been mostly a patriarchal culture in the US, and the vast majority of the population still are patriarchal cultures. We have built our structures on power, control, and hierarchy, all for the sake of producing, controlling, and power. We have forfeited our ability to live in harmony with our planet because we are so focused in the mind about conquering nature for the sake of profit.

The divine feminine energies are considered weak in our society. They are considered less than or unwanted with employers and at the workspace. Think about your office and how divine feminine energies are looked upon. Statements like, "This is work, leave your personal life and emotions at home," and "Keep your emotions in check," are common. If you are in a male dominated workspace, the male jargon that attacks one's maleness with female adjectives. Although, they are not gender specific, the energies do lend themselves to the gender roles. Think about what demographic is typically paid less, mistreated, abused, and sexually assaulted. In addition, how do we look at the entire family dynamic? In our society, females have generally been underpaid and recognized as less than in the workplace compared to males.

Let us go back to your childhood. The vast majority of you have been taught that doing something has been the way to add value to your life. We are told to act a certain way to be rewarded with love. We are told that to be a valued part of society requires you to contribute through action and results. In addition, it is reinforced that your emotions are not valid and only those that make others happy are what you should feel. We are taught only competition and winning bring you joy and happiness. We are reinforced through the competition with accolades and trophies.

In our current education system, the grade schools are giving grades for results of doing and action. We further "grade" children's abilities to do things and they are awarded for results that display outperformance. Although some of the energies of the divine feminine are honored, the majority of the teaching is around divine masculine. We must get a high GPA and do many different activities to get into a college or university. Then we must succeed at that to get a good job that pays well. Entering yet another masculine hierarchy program of doing, producing, and results.

Look further into the society structures we are living in. We have the monetary system, the financial system, the health care system, the education system, etc. They are centered on hierarchy and reinforcement of results, producing, control, and competition. Our society is a manifestation of the divine masculine energies.

I am not saying the divine masculine is bad or evil. I am saying we are wildly unbalanced toward masculine energy. Within our own selves we focus on doing, producing, and acting without honoring the divine feminine energies. We are imbalanced within these energies and therefore our creations are as well. This perpetuates the energetics as the creator, and we continue to manifest the unbalanced pattens within our reality and that of our human collective.

How can you create peace, love, and joy out of energy that is imbalanced with hurt, fear, and rejection? When we decide to act, produce, and create without honoring where our energies come from, we create experiences that are heavily bias toward the divine masculine while repressing the divine feminine. Forcing action through divine masculine is repressing the divine feminine. Action over feelings. The emotional body or the divine feminine is shut down, repressed, and rejected. Since we know the law of attraction will generate experiences based on what you are holding on to, we continue the reality we are having. The Universe will continue to reflect the repressed energies. The energies will further press upon you until you become aware of it and rebalance the energy.

We must start honoring the divine feminine energies to balance. We must attune to our beings and honor the two energies within us first. This will help us understand and honor our emotions to create balance within us and ultimately in our society.

## EMOTIONS ARE IMPORTANT

We are told that emotions are not important. The majority of our lives we are told to act in accordance with what pleases our parents or other people. It is only recently that we are seeing a slight shift to validating our emotions in mainstream parenting. We are understanding how emotions are powerful. They are powerful tools for understanding who we are rather than useless biproducts of being human. The human emotional response is an energetic signal about your beliefs. To deny your human emotional response is to deny your humanity.

The majority of us are taught incorrectly about our emotions. We have been through an archaic education system that told, scolded, and reinforced us into believing that our emotions are false. That to be loved we must act in a certain accordance to what our parents, peers, and other beings expect us to be. A perfectly behaved person that doesn't cause others to feel any dissonance other than joy and happiness. Don't show any negative emotions and be perfect. What is negative? What is perfect? These are all individual perspectives that we decided to repress in ourselves to conform to someone else's need of love and security. Someone else's desires . . . not yours.

Think about our current society, especially when it comes to employment. The identity for the majority is to repress our emotions or leave our feelings at home. The place of employment is for productivity and results. There is no place for your personal emotional baggage, and one should leave that at home. Emotions are looked upon as a weakness and vehemently rejected. They are something to reject because they get in the way of productivity and business profitability.

We are constantly downplaying or discounting people for their emotions. How about when you are feeling emotions and crying out for attention? Have any of you been called "a cry baby"? Have any of you called someone else that? We have conditioned ourselves to believe that crying and showing our emotions make us into a baby or that we are in an infantile state of being. It shames the person, and as many do when responding to being called a "cry baby," they repress the emotions and act like nothing was wrong.

We must understand that our emotions are to be honored. Emotions are not something that should be conquered or something that are useless aspects to us. It is part of being human. It is a beautiful part of being human. The range of emotions that we go through are intense and capricious. This is what makes the human experience so valuable. It is an intense way of understanding yourself as Source. You get to have all these emotions and extremes of emotions, which catalyze you to know how deep that love can be for yourself. Your emotions are powerful and when you do not honor them it can cause havoc. As mentioned before, honoring your divine feminine energy it is needed to balance out the energies. Emotions are part of your divine feminine energies. Emotions are fundamental to understanding yourself.

Your emotions are needed as biological feedback for you to understand yourself and the things that you are creating. They are your way to understand that your reality is in alignment or out of alignment with what you want. They are essential to the human experience and being the creator. Emotions are your tool for interpreting the reality you are creating, and they help you create your reality at the same time. If you knew how important your emotions are in relation to the whole, you would be more inclined to monitor your emotions like a treasure.

Emotions are the causes for many illnesses in the body. The natural state of your vibrational energy seeks to find ease and harmony. When you reject emotions, you throw your energetics off. Repressed or rejected emotions cause dis-ease and dis-harmony in your energetic field. The physical follows suit. The physical is a lagging effect of the energy. A dis-ease and dis-harmonious energy field creates a body that matches. The body becomes diseased and disharmonious, leading to aging, illness, and ultimately death. Emotions are integral to your energy system.

The feedback system of your emotions is pretty simple. Typically, feelings that are in alignment with your desires as a creator are characterized as:

- Joy
- Passionate
- Loving
- Happy
- Blissful
- Peaceful

Emotions that do not align with your desires as the creator are characterized as:

- Anger
- Sadness
- Depression
- Boredom
- Anxiety
- Stress
- Fear

When you feel emotions that are in alignment as the creator, you are expressing joy and happiness. There is no question as to why this brings you happiness. You continue to do what you are doing because it is bringing you joy and happiness. It is a sign or feedback from your emotions that what you are creating is in alignment with your intentions. It feels good and you do more of it.

When you feel the emotions that are not in alignment with you as the creator, you are expressing emotions to show that. Most likely anger, frustration, anxiety, stress, etc. The vast majority of people try to avoid these feelings or find a way to cope with them. Since we are taught to reject emotions or to treat them as not valuable aspects of us, we ignore them. We never question why we are feeling those emotions. Without understanding why they come about or how they come about, we move along in another direction or continue to repeat the same experience. We completely reject the emotional signal, "Hey creator, this doesn't feel good." The signal gets broadcasted but we ignore it, never changing anything about ourselves. We are then destined to relive the emotional experience yet again because it was repressed and rejected.

Most of us categorize emotions that are not in alignment as "negative" or "bad." We think it is a bad thing to have emotions like anger. I do not agree with this. I think emotions are emotions, they are all good. You need them all! Emotions are your feedback. Why separate your emotions as good or bad when they are all giving you feedback on your reality? This leads us to repress or avoid feelings that are considered *negative* emotions. Even though they are trying to tell you that you do not like this!! We have been taught incorrectly about our emotions. All emotions are valid. Neither good nor bad. They are just signals to you as the creator. Your emotions are what tell you that you should explore more of this or that, or that what you are creating is not in alignment with you.

Let us take a moment to discuss the emotion of anger. Anger is likely what many of you are dealing with. Anger is a coping mechanism for your trauma. It is an emotion you have before you get to your core. Almost like a protective mother over a vulnerable child.

If you are a parent, then you can understand the idea of "Don't poke the momma bear!" My wife and I joke about this all the time, but there is truth to this statement. "Don't poke the momma bear" is referencing the idea that she will rear up, show her teeth, and slash her claws if tested. The main reason is because of her cubs. A parent or momma bear is protective over her cubs or children. When their safety or overall well-being is threatened, then momma bear gets angry and will fight. She will come to their defense.

In this metaphor, the cubs or the children are underlying traumas such as feeling hurt, powerless, and unloved. Momma bear will rear up and show her teeth in an angry defense. When you begin to feel the underlying pain, or feel threatened to feel them, the angry momma bear comes out. You will get angry to protect yourself from feeling these other things. Anger is not the final emotion. It is the last stop before you get to the underlying core feeling.

Anger is not the true emotion that you are trying to understand. Anger is a protective emotion. It is the gate keeper emotion before you get to the real issue. If you are dealing with a lot of anger, it is important for you to find out what your cubs are. What is the true reason for why you are angry? This is for you to find out for yourself. Just remember that when you feel anger or you are feeling angry, you are poking the momma bear. Momma bear that is protecting other emotions from being felt.

## YOUR EMOTIONS AND HOW THEY ARE BEING USED

As a young child, you are brought into a reality that is deeply dependent on your parents. You rely on them to get you through this physical dimension and understanding your senses. You also rely on them to teach you about your emotions. Let's say you were playing as child. You may have felt an emotion, such as joy, as you played. You were learning to express an emotion, or to express something energetically from within you. If your parents were to find your emotional expression did not align with them, then there would be a dissonance within you. You would be told the emotion was not something that should be felt and reprimanded for it. You would internalize that emotion or the energy as a negative energy. *Feeling this certain emotion should be rejected because I do not receive love when I express it.* You would begin to repress the emotion as you move forward. Anytime that emotion or energy shows up, you would reject it. In place of that, you would search for what your parents would deem acceptable in their perspective. You would then try to hold the accepted response and energy that your parents desired. Being happy and not whining or crying or any emotions that did not fit with their wants.

What is happening energetically when this happens? As the creator, you are expressing an emotion. If that emotion is rejected, then the emotion was never expressed. You had energy swell up from the depths within you to be expressed but then you repressed it back down. It was never expressed and released outwardly. When your emotions are rejected, they get stuck within your energy field and become part of it. The repressed emotion becomes part of you. It becomes part of the energy you create from. The repressed energy adds to the sum of your vibration, the frequency you put out into the Universe. If your emotion was not rejected, you had someone who validated the emotion and allowed you to express the energy, it would not have gotten stuck within your energy field.

Energy you never let go of or energy that was never expressed becomes an energy imprint. That energy imprint becomes part of the overall energy that you create from. Think about a printing press here. You have a basic design for your print. You start printing copies, and all is well. Then you go about life and suddenly you get a repressed emotion. That repressed emotion is like changing the original print design from which copies are being made. It distorts copies going forward. It would be like adding a new image onto your design that does not belong there. Now, new copies are being made with an erroneous image. Leaving you with distorted prints of your original design. Like the printing press, the repressed energy will repeat over and over in your life. It makes copies of your imprint throughout your life. These repressed emotions or feeling are patterning out everywhere. The patterns are there to reinforce the rejected and repressed emotion. This is why your emotions are so important to you. If you do not honor them, you are creating a pattern of yourself with all sorts of distortions. Most of these distortions are emotions rejected by those you are dependent on.

As a child I was beaten for wanting attention. I was about three or four years old, and any parent knows that at that age children test boundaries. Children seek to understand themselves and their emotions. In times of distress, I would call out to my parents that I needed help, assistance, attention, or something to feel loved in the moment. My father, enraged by my action, beat me for it. The outcry for love was rejected. Leaving me feeling pained, hurt, and deeply saddened. I learned not to accept myself and my emotions because they were rejected. I was beaten for feeling. The natural impulse was to adjust myself to avoid feeling this pain. I would adjust my entire energetic field to appease the being of my father. Any time I would sense that emotion, I would adjust it by numbing, repressing, and lashing out in anger just to avoid feeling that pain again.

This was my pattern in my life. A deep seeded pain and longing for love that would be protected by my anger. I would lash out whenever someone came close to this pain, and I would destroy all in its path. Anger was a powerful emotion within me. I dealt with a lot of anger in my life.

## EMOTIONAL HIJACKING

Hijacking occurs because many of us are unconscious of ourselves. It happens primarily because our emotional body is completely out of synch, and we have repressed emotions that open us up to hijacking. Emotional hijacking is a common theme and is used on us on a daily basis. Hijacking is typically associated with someone seizing control of the vehicle without permission or by force. The subsequent vehicle is then used for the intent and purpose of the hijacker.

The hijacking I am talking about is not as forceful as taking over a vehicle. It is more of a passive permission to allow someone to take over the wheel. No force needed. The hijacker pretends they are doing the best things for you, and you give them permission to do what they please. How is this done? It is done because you gave your power away due to fear.

For the most part, many of us are repressing our emotions. We fear our repressed emotions and fear seeing the rejected aspects of ourselves. We do whatever we can to not feel these emotions. We try our best to avoid them. By doing so, we give our power away to anything or anyone to help us avoid them.

For example, I have self-worth issues stemming from my abusive father. To avoid this feeling, I tried to feel love and acceptance through friendships and other romantic relationship. I accepted social norms to feel part of something and loved. If a group or person told me to do something, I would follow suit. I would do so even if it were not for my highest good. This is because of the fear of feeling rejected. I feared feeling unloved and unworthy so much that I would rather cave to peer pressure to appease my friends. Peer pressure is a powerful thing to someone who is unconscious about themselves.

This is how emotional hijacking can occur in a personal micro sense. We deal with this all the time in our relationships and co-created experiences. If you expand emotional hijacking to the collective, in a macro sense, you can see how insidious it is. A prime example of emotional hijacking can be seen with the use of media. Movies, television, and radio have all used emotional hijacking to get us to do things, buy things, or believe in certain narratives. Think about all the advertisements that use your repressed emotions to get you buy something. Movies and television utilize images and stories that are projected onto you all the time. Music and music videos do the same thing. They broadcast a vibration into your reality in hopes it resonates with you. There are constant bombardments of projected vibrations all around you about what is considered socially accepted from the content creators. Body image, sex, and money are constantly thrown in your face and we give our power to it. They play on your repressed emotions and the fear you have around seeing and feeling them.

When you are emotionally repressed, say, around self-worth issues, you will follow along with what is projected at you. This is because you fear what you reject about yourself. You do not want to be rejected. The media will project a version of success into your reality. It will show success as having lots of money, so much you can throw it carelessly around. There are big yachts and big homes and fancy cars. They are surrounded by people wearing expensive clothes and jewelry. This makes you feel less than and presses upon your self-worth issues. They know how to play on your fears. Since you are emotionally imbalanced you will give up your power to feel the opposite. This leads you to try to fit in, to buy the clothes and get rich. You are volunteering yourself to be hijacked into doing what they want you to do. In the end, you lose your sense of self and who you are. You are not authentic and find yourself not knowing who you are.

I used to think that success was wearing expensive suits, having a nice car, and making lots of money. I was hijacked by what others were doing and what I saw in the media. I took on what other people thought was success. I would hold myself out there as someone who was put together and had their head on their shoulders. I pretended to be something I was not, and it did not make me feel peaceful or happy.

In truth, I was barely holding on. I was a loose cannon emotionally and I feared myself. I feared feeling unloved and feeling rejected. I tried to be something I was not because of my emotional state. I was scared of being me because I felt being me was not good enough. All my power was given away because I did not want to face my emotions.

This process of becoming the creator is a process to sovereignty. It is a process to reclaim what rightfully belongs to you. Through self-love and connecting deeply with what you are, you will heal. This begins with understanding that your emotions are valid and need to be honored. You will find balance with your emotions when you begin to honor them. It will help you become sovereign and powerful. Then you can watch in amazement how these low vibrational hijacking energies fall off you as they no longer serve you as the creator.

## ENERGY CAN BE STORED IN THE BODY

The body can become a holding container for repressed energy. When you have powerful emotions from traumatic experiences, you may unconsciously store the emotional energy in your body. Since you never let the energy out, the energy must go somewhere. It most cases it stays in the body. The energy moves into the cells within your body and is held there until you can release it. Until that time, your body will continue to remind you that you have it stored within it.

The body reminds you that you have densities of repressed emotions. Little reminders from the body that say, "Hey, you have something here and it needs to be released." Unfortunately, the body does not have linear human communication to convey something that it is holding on to. It must create a message that the creator can see or feel. These reminders may look or feel like physical pain or discomfort, weight gain, stiffness, or any other form of bodily disease of disharmonious states. It may create certain movements as a way to inform you of the energy.

For instance, my body reacts to feeling unsafe in a certain way. I will have an urge to want to get up and run out. I want to leave. When confronted with an experience of feeling unloved or rejection, my body starts to communicate to me. I will have a strong urge to leave and pace around. I want to run from the pain of feeling unloved or rejected.

I recall many times where I was in a heated shouting match with my wife. I could sense this feeling and I became aware that I was pacing around my house. No direction, just anywhere but here. This was an indication I had energy stored within the body and it was trying to show me. The body was almost moving on its own, but I never got the message because I did not know how to communicate with it.

When I was single, in my late 20s, and renting a room in a friend's house, I was dealing with a lot of different energies. I had recently joined a new financial firm and was barely making ends meet. I was constantly worried about money and stressed out about the job. I was getting into the shower one day and suddenly I felt an intense pain in my lower back. I realized I pulled my back and could hardly move. In agonizing pain, I limped out of the shower and was barely able to get dressed for medical help. I managed to get over it with prescription pain medicine and a few days on the couch. A few years later when I was getting ready to go on a honeymoon with my wife, I dealt with the exact same back injury. I was worried because we were spending money on a trip right after we bought our first house together. I decided it was a good idea to go to the gym the day before our flight to feel good. I pushed myself on an exercise and injured myself again. I spent the next few days on our honeymoon completely uncomfortable and consuming pain medications. When I look back on that injury, all the signs were there. I was dealing with repressed emotions that were stored in my lower back. I was refusing to look at not feeling safe, not feeling like we had enough money, and self-worth issues. In addition, I felt like I was unsupported and never expressed it.

Your emotions are to be honored and accepted as part of you. Emotions are important to you. They just do not communicate in a linear way. It takes time and openness to listen to what your body is trying to tell you. So how can we get an insight into the way the body communicates? Through the energy centers call the *chakras*.

## THE BASIC SEVEN CHAKRAS

As a Reiki master, I would be remiss if I did not review or introduce the basic chakra system. The chakra system is vitally important to you as the creator. Fortunately, the esoteric information of the chakra system is a bit more mainstream these days. Yogis and other healing modalities have allowed for the information about chakras to be a familiar concept. People know more about them and can at least hold on to the information compared to in the past.

There are far more detailed books on chakras and their function than what this volume of text will cover. I recommend searching for more information should this information peak your interest. For now, we need to be on the same level of understanding so that we can get a basic function understood.

Imagine, if you will, you are back in your high school science class. Your teacher turns off the lights in the room and shines a beam of white light into a prism. What do you witness? You see white light separated out into the colors of the rainbow, or ROYGBIV. ROYGBIV is an acronym for each color of the rainbow; red, orange, yellow, green, blue, indigo, and violet. In an oversimplification, that is what the chakra system is. It is light and sound broken out into separate colors. Your chakras are basically the separated energetics of Source light manifested into a network that has tangible and viable information for you to understand about yourself. The chakras are a feedback system for you as the creator.

There are seven basic energy centers of the chakra system. Each energy center is located along the spine from the top of your head to the base of your spine. The centers are not exactly on the spine but give you an idea about location. It is also important to note that hierarchy does not denote level of importance, for the first energy center is just as important as the last and vice versa. Hierarchy is used to describe location within the body and their relationships. Each energy center corresponds to different awareness about yourself.

**The Root:** The Sanskrit word for the root is *Muladhara*. The root chakra is located at the base of the spine. The color associated with the root is red. Its relationship to you as the creator is the entry point for which the prana of the world enters. Much like a tree, the root system is integral to drawing nutrients and creates a solid foundation within the soil. It is important to establish a strong root system if you plan on growing into a large, tall tree. Your root chakra is primarily related to your awareness of meeting your materialistic needs of the physical world. It is your survival in the physical world and dealing with the fight or flight response. You are looking to establish security around food, shelter, clothes, money, etc. The root governs your adrenal and is mostly related to the physical body parts of the colon, rectum, prostate, and legs. If you have a block or dysfunction here you can experience lower back pain, sciatica, varicose veins, depression, insecurity, stability issues, stress, and/or focus on material possessions.

**The Sacral:** The Sanskrit word for sacral is *Svadhisthana*. The sacral is the second chakra located just below the belly button (about the width of two fingers). The color associated with the sacral is orange. Your relationship to the sacral is about self-discovery. After meeting your basic materialistic needs of the physical world, a being can begin to spend time and energy in the exploration of self. The sacral chakra is the energy center for emotions, desires, and sexuality. It is the center for you to understand yourself. The sacral is related to the reproductive and digestive areas of your body. If you have blocks or dysfunction here you can experience lower back pain, sciatica, urinary issues, low libido, emotional imbalance, lack of motivation, digestive issues, kidney issues, gonads/testes issues, and/or ovaries issues.

**The Solar Plexus**: The Sanskrit word for the solar plexus is *Manipura*. The solar plexus is the third chakra located about where your rib cage curves. The color associated with the solar plexus is yellow. As one evolves their energy and awareness about themselves, they can expend their energy on the social construct of their reality. This center deals with power and authority that arise from one's social or societal environments, such as social groups, government, work environment, etc. The physical body parts related to the solar plexus are around the pancreas which governs the liver, digestive system, stomach, spleen, gall bladder, lower back, and muscles. Blocks or dysfunctions can cause diabetes, liver issues, skin issues, indigestion, anger issues, dominance issues, and gut issues.

**The Heart:** The Sanskrit word for the heart chakra is *Anahata*. The heart is the fourth chakra located in the middle of your chest where your physical heart is. The heart chakra is the energy center associated with compassion, beauty, and love, especially that of unconditional love. This is the middle point or bridge between the physical and the spiritual energy centers. The physical related chakras being the lower three chakras. The more etheric or spiritual chakras being the next higher three chakras. The heart center relates to being able to fully accept and love all that Source created. The associated body parts are related to the thymus that governs the heart, lungs, blood circulation, ribs, breast, upper back, arms, and hands. Blocks or dysfunction here can cause asthma, lung and breast issues, pneumonia, upper back issues, shoulder issues, heart issues, difficulties in giving and receiving love, and feeling standoffish.

**The Throat:** The Sanskrit word for the throat chakra is *Vishuddha*. The throat is the fifth chakra located in the center of your neck, or where your throat is. We associate the throat with your vocal cords and sound. This chakra is the first step into the more spiritual and etheric realm of your reality. The color associate with this chakra is blue. The energy center is related to the ideas around truth and communication. As you rise above the physical realm platforms, one seeks to know the truth of themselves and that of the world. Here one seeks the truth beyond that of time and space. The body parts associated with the throat are the thyroid which governs the jaw, mouth, gums, neck, trachea, voice, airways, shoulders, and arms. Blocks or dysfunction here can cause sore throat, anemia, allergies, voice issues, gum and tooth issues, mouth issues, TMJ, difficulties with personal expression, and being overly critical of others and yourself.

**The Third Eye:** The Sanskrit word for the third eye chakra is *Ajna*. The third eye is the sixth chakra located at the brow of your head. The color associated with this chakra is indigo/navy blue. Here we are dealing with intuition and foresight. It is the mental aspect of you and what we closely associate as the "clair" abilities: clairsentient, clairvoyant, clairaudient, claircognizant, and clairgustance. This is about the mind, body, and spirit moving through space and time. This is not only about balance within self, but also the balance with Source. It is the link to intelligence Source. The body parts associated with the third eye are the pituitary gland that governs the eyes, ears, nose, sinuses, brain, and nervous system. Blocks or dysfunction can cause brain tumors, headaches, eye issues, ear issues, nose issues, mental disabilities or issues, feelings of panic, judgement, cloudy thinking, lack of focus, and fear of the truth.

**The Crown:** The Sanskrit word for the crown chakra is *Sahasrara*. The crown is the seventh and the last chakra of the basic seven chakras outlined here. It is located at the top of your head. This is the sum of all the other chakras. Much like a thermometer in the water, the crown is the measure of the sum of all the energy within the chakras. The body part associated with the crown is the pineal gland where melatonin is produced. Blocks or dysfunction here can cause light sensitivity, sound sensitivity, environmental sensitivity, nervous system and head issues.

These are the basic seven chakras that make up your energy feedback system. You can relate many illnesses within the body to a block or distortion in the chakras. You can even get insight into what your traumas are if you are open to understanding the chakras. Knowledge of the chakras can provide great insight into all areas of your life. This is especially true with beliefs you are holding on to.

For instance, if you are dealing with anxiety, you may have issues with your root chakra. The root chakra deals with feeling safe and getting physical needs met. When you do not feel safe, you do not want to be in the present moment. It makes you feel unsafe in the body. You cannot help but feel the anxiety and the fear of what may happen. You exert all this energy trying to feel safe. This may leave you completely drained and exhausted because you are literally fighting with yourself.

The distortion in your root chakra is not allowing the energy to move upward into the other chakras. The energy will not flow naturally. It is being pinched off at the root chakra. The block is forcing your attention and energy to be stuck in the root. The root is about meeting your material and physical needs. It is about safety and security. The chances are you would also develop some type of physical issue with the body around root, especially with your legs. If you do not know what is causing your anxiety, you could get insight from the chakras specific to the root.

Many of us are living in a constant state of fear. Fear distorts your chakras and the energy that runs through you. Fear restricts your energy centers from flowing freely in and out. One of the biggest blocks to your chakras are rejected energies, especially with regards to emotions. When you reject an energy, that energy is not allowed to be expressed. It gets stuck. The energy is held in place looking for a place to go. It gets stored somewhere. It gets stored in the body.

This is vitally important with regards to emotional energy and your chakras. Several physical issues can be attributed to a rejected emotion. If you can, imagine that you have a blueprint for your body. Just like an architect creates a blueprint for constructing a building, your physical body follows a blueprint. This blueprint is made up of moving light. When you have a repressed emotion, it is like taking a sluggish slow energy and slabbing it all over your blueprint. The sluggish energy affects the light in your blueprint, and everything slows down or gets distorted.

The physical body will follow the blueprint that you have in place. It has no other option but to reflect the blueprint. Much like builders who construct a house, they follow the blueprint laid out before them. They have no other option because that is what the blueprint says for them to do. Your physical body is much the same way. It will construct your body based on the blueprint you hold. If that blueprint has sluggish guck all over it, the body will manifest health or physical issues to reflect the energy. It will reflect health issues to bring awareness to the rejected or repressed emotion bleeding all over your blueprint. A way to see into the blueprint and what is going on is to use the chakras as a tool.

The body will reflect physical issues that corresponds with the energy center that the distortion was created from. For instance, let us say you are having knee issues on the right leg. That is an indication that you are holding onto root chakra problems. This could be about movement, feeling safe, about not feeling safe to take action, etc. Chakras are a feedback system, along with your physical body, to reflect things about yourself.

As discussed in the previous chapter, there is a mirror that can be experienced through the chakra system. What you are experiencing in the physical world, from power struggles to physical pain, can be mirrored back to you through the chakra system. It just takes time and practice to understand it. It takes practice to bring awareness to your chakras and body.

Chakra Awareness Mediation:

## *Get into a meditative state (see Meditation section in Chapter 7).*

*Use your mind to drop into your root. Imagine a light dropping from your head down to the root chakra, drawing your attention into the energy center. If that is difficult to imagine, then place your physical hands on your root area and connect that with touch. Now, imagine a red door in front of you. Whatever door is to your liking. Reach out to open the door. As the door opens, imagine a red light spilling out from inside. What color red are you seeing? Is the red pale, is it bright, does it look weak, or does it look strong? Now walk through the door into the root chakra room. What exists in that room? What do you see in the room? Explore the space. There are things in here for you to see and interpret. When you feel called to leave, send a loving golden light into the room as you walk out and close the door.*

*Repeat for each chakra.*

*Many of us do not feel safe within the body. We are in a constant state of fear which keeps us from being in the moment. We are either thinking about the past and trying to avoid pain or remember good times or we are in the future worried about what could be. The constant fear makes us feel anxious, stressed, depressed,* and emotionally imbalanced. Our thoughts are all over the place. You cannot focus, you are perseverating on fearful or concerning thoughts. This all affects our physical bodies. As you know, when you are in a fearful state your breathing gets shallow and your heartrate picks up. It is the fight or flight reaction, and your body goes into hyperdrive. Adrenaline is pumped and everything is heightened. Long periods of this can be disastrous to us and has proven to be so. We feel unsafe within the body.

To help you anchor back into your body, you need to bring awareness back to it. You need to ground back in. Here is an exercise to help you reign in the fear and start getting back into the body.

## Grounding into Body Exercise (10-15 minutes):

Sit and close your eyes. Focus on your breath. Breathe in nice and deep. In through the nose and out through the mouth. Breath deep into your abdomen. This helps calm the vagus nerve and relieve the fight or flight sensation. Focus on your breath entering the body and exiting the body for a few minutes. Start to notice how your body feels. Can you feel your heartbeat? Notice if you are holding any tension? Notice the sensations of your body. Notice how the air feels. Notice the pressure from sitting in your body. Notice how your clothes feel.

What sounds do you hear? What noises are around you?

What can you smell? What aromas are around you?

What can you taste?

Open your eyes and start to notice the body. The position that you are in. The colors that are around you.

# CHAPTER 5:
# START FREEING YOURSELF

I was standing in my living room, livid, staring down at my daughter as she was crying hysterically on the floor. I had just yelled at her for not listening to me and I had physically pushed her away from the tablet I told her not to touch. My wife came running to her aid to offer love and to try to help her feel safe again. My daughter was about the same age that I was when all my trauma occurred. My daughter was hurt by how I treated her, and my wife was appalled at my actions and behavior. It was a major wake up call to me.

I was angry. I saw my father in the moment. I had become what I told myself I would not become. I had so many different emotions running through me. The anger projected at both my wife and daughter. I was angry at myself. Then came the shame and the guilt. I was feeling absolutely disgusted with myself. I did not want to be myself. I wanted to run away.

I wanted to free myself of this feeling. The thing I hated most about myself was staring right back at me through the experience of my daughter and wife. It catalyzed me to seek inward and heal. To free myself of the vibrational patterns that I was holding on to. This was all magnetized into my reality as the creator because I needed to be catalyzed. It was time for me to awaken to the limited beliefs I was holding on to.

We are about to embark into the unknown adventure that lays within you. Here we are seeking to understand the things we do not understand or are unconscious of about ourselves. To become conscious of the darkness that is within that seeks to be seen. It is a process of awareness to understand why things are the way they are. You are about to dive deep into yourself and adventure around the many parts of you that have been hidden and keeping you enslaved.

It is time to free yourself of the patterns that no longer serve you as the creator. It is time to see that you have been wearing shackles on your wrists and ankles. The shackles are self-imposed, and you must be able to see you had the key all along. You must see that you have limited yourself and kept yourself small. You have kept yourself contained and from feeling more peaceful in your life.

You have new tools and knowledge now. What you have learned provides a path to move forward. With newly acquired tools we can freely move to accomplish our task at hand. It took me many experiences to be catalyzed into awareness. I banged my head against the same wall and got nowhere. I had to truly understand why my patterns kept happening. This means we must start bringing awareness to ourselves. To start bringing our unconsciousness into the light and becoming conscious about what has been in the dark.

Many of you are like the computers that we use daily. I have no background on computer programming or any other technical knowledge around the hardware or software that is used to run a computer. I am aware of them, but I am only conscious of the programs I that use. I am aware of the few programs that are needed for me to get my work done, such as my internet browser and the programs used to type up this book. What I am unaware of are the programs used to run the computer. I have no idea what is keeping this computer operating.

Your reality is like a computer. You are aware of only a few programs needed to get through your day. You only know of a few surface programs, but you are unaware of the underlying programs that are running your computer. You are unconscious of what programs are contributing to the overall performance and well-being of the computer. Even more shocking is that many of us are running our computer without any idea that we have a virus infecting us.

What happens when we get a virus on our computer? Our computer slows down. We get pop-ups and random screens. Things become corrupt or we cannot use other programs properly. You turn your computer on and it gives you indications something is wrong. As a computer user, you would notice all these red flags that something is not right. There are obvious signs or signals that it is time to act and clean things out.

It is incredulous that many of us do not do that. We go through life and get these red flag experiences that are like virus pop-ups on our computer. We stare them right in the face, but we end up ignoring them completely. We remain destructively ignorant of these red flags and go about our day like nothing is wrong. Our computer is screaming at us like a big flashing red neon sign that says, "Warning!" It is flashing and blaring, but we shrug our shoulders and blame the world. We blame external things for our problems. It was their fault, and they are causing me this suffering. The world becomes the scapegoat for how our life is going. Not realizing we are one hundred percent accountable for what is occurring in our lives.

My life had so many red flags or warnings. I just could not see them for what they were. Some were blatantly in my face and I missed them all because I was unconscious of it. I cannot tell you the number of times my wife said to me that I was an angry person. I remember after a heated exchange she turned to me and said, "You need to see someone! You are so angry." Each time she said that to me, I felt she was wrong. I would return with a glare of disbelief that she had the audacity to say such a thing. There was nothing wrong with me, it was all her. Except she was right. I was in denial and I was completely oblivious to it. It took a big catalyst for me to say enough is enough and to wake up to what I was creating in my life.

## BECOME AWARE OF YOURSELF

There is an old saying, "How do you free someone who doesn't know they are a slave?" It never serves to tell someone that they are suffering from their own enslavement. It is best to show them how different their life could be. You must show them that they have been a slave this whole time. It is time to see that you have been a slave of your own making. Let us stop this everyday nonsense and start freeing ourselves. This part of the journey is about bringing awareness to yourself and making changes from what we learn.

Imagine your reality is like a calm body of water. Imagine that each thought you have is like throwing a rock into the water. You take a rock and throw it into the water. The rock splashes into the calm water and it ripples outward. A wave of energy moves through the surface. The rippling effect is the consequence of that thought and we observe it rippling through our reality.

Most of us are unconsciously throwing rocks into our own body of water. These rocks are covered with energy that we are holdings on to. Rocks that contain fear, hurt, pain, anger, and other low vibrational energies. Then when we see the ripple effect of the rocks, we look at our experience and blame others for how it went. Most never look at themselves and ask why their reality is like what it is.

You are responsible for the rocks you throw into your water. No one else. You feel disempowered right now, but you are the only one that is in control of your life. You are accountable for the ripple effect within your reality. It is thrust upon you to determine what rocks you would like to throw into that water. The process outlined here is to become conscious of the rocks you are throwing into your own body of water.

We must self-examine ourselves. Brutal honesty is required here. It is vitally important that you are honest with yourself. Without honesty you will not get to the core of yourself. Bear in mind that sometimes we can lie to ourselves without knowing we are. The truth can get mixed up in our head. We can believe in illusions and the unbelievable lies we tell ourselves. This is why I say focus on your emotions and how you feel. Feelings and emotions do not lie. They lead you to the truth. Your mind and ego can lie to you. It has lied to you this whole time. If you are like me, you have believed a lie for the last thirty years. What does this tell you? You have created many ways to hide yourself from the truth. Mentally and logically thinking your way out of it may not be the best way to free yourself. You need your emotions to help you navigate this work.

## Awareness Exercise 1: Remember a Triggering Experience

If you are reading this book, the likelihood is that you are dealing with some level of pain that you would like to get away from. Something that you want to change. To change something, you must first be able understand that you have a problem in the first place.

The easiest place to start is to take the most recent event or experience that made you feel "negative" emotions. I want you to try and remember or recall the experience to its fullest extent. Try to remember everything like you are reliving the situation again, but I want you to pay particular attention to:

- Your emotions
- What was said to you
- What was done to you
- How it made you feel
- What the environment looked like
- What you were thinking

Example: I recall a huge argument with my wife about our kitchen after we recently purchased our house. I was standing near the sink and my wife was standing between the barstools on the other side of the island. It was mid-day, and the light was coming through the small kitchen window. She said she wanted to repaint the cabinets and walls and change out the countertops and kitchen light fixtures. I remember getting really angry. I was almost furious. I remember thinking we did not have the money and that nothing was ever good enough for her. I remember thinking that this kitchen was better than anything I had ever had. I remember thinking that I worked so hard and put my money into this house. I remembered yelling, "Can't you just be happy with what we have? You're never happy with what we've got!" I was aggressively pointing at her. I wanted to walk away and felt like I needed to move.

At this point you may want to write down things that really come to mind. For me it was:

- I was angry about her wanting to change things.
- Things were never good enough.
- I felt like I had no power.
- I wanted to walk away.
- I was yelling at her.
- It felt like the house was not good enough.

## Awareness Exercise 2: Identifying the Pattern

Hopefully the first awareness exercise opened your eyes to the fact that there are misaligned experiences. That there are things showing up but perhaps we have not thought deep enough about them. Perhaps you thought that they were just everyday life and there was no need to look further.

This is far from the truth. When you keep having the same emotions brought about by different experiences, it is a sign for us to look into. We are being shown by our reality that there is something there. It is more than a coincidence if it happens more than once. There is an intention happening behind the scenes and your energy is trying to tell you something. It is trying to show what got inside you.

Let us take this exercise a little further and see if this is just a one-time occurrence.

Repeat Awareness Exercise 1. This time I want you to bring up a different memory where you experienced something negative in your life. What were the details about that experience? Notice any similarities between this experience and the first experience. Pay particular attention to the emotions being expressed.

Repeat this as many times as you wish.

There can be a lot of information that can be extracted from one negative memory. These negative moments are gateways for us to see right into the depth of hidden trauma or pain that we refused to look at. It takes a little courage to look around. We need to inquire to see if there is a problem. We need to know about the "why." We need to understand why we are feeling what we are feeling from our experiences. What is causing us to constantly have these emotions come up in our reality.

It is important to state that if the finger is not pointing at you by the end of this exercise, then you do not have the right answer. The answer is always you. You are the creator, and you must take accountability for what has happened. It is easy to say the reason for you feeling this or that is because of something outside of you. That is the easy answer, but there is more to it. If you are blaming someone else, then start over and try again until the finger is pointing at you. This is especially true for experiences with another person. Remember that co-creators are mirrors. You must see yourself in the mirror.

On the surface, it can seem obvious as to what may be going on. Remember in Chapter 4 about anger and "don't poke momma bear." If you are feeling anger, there is more to the picture. From my example above, I was clearly angry at my wife for saying she wanting to update the kitchen. I was angry about all sorts of things but why was I angry? What is my anger protecting? What was my anger about? I was angry because I felt hurt and unworthy. I felt like I was not good enough because I projected my self-worth on the house. I was angry because I felt like a victim. When my wife wanted to change things around it felt like I was being attacked or that I was not good enough. I felt like a victim and powerless.

Go through this exercise enough times and we can start to see that there is an underlying pattern. In my example, I can see there is a pattern of feeling unworthy, I have self-worth issues, and I have power issues. I get angry because I do not want to feel unworthy. I get angry because I feel like I am a victim and I want power. Ultimately, it makes me feel unloved and it brings up so much pain. There is a lot of anger patterning out in my life.

Remember that once an imprint has taken place, it will make copies of itself all the time, in many different areas of your life. This core imprint does not just compartmentalize itself in only one aspect of your life. It will show up everywhere.

## Awareness Exercise 3: Understand the Belief

Now you are aware there is a pattern happening in your life. You have to start to understand where this pattern lives. You must understand how widespread the problem is. You must understand where this belief has gotten its way into everything. The belief has kept you where you are, and you are not able to see outside of the box it has put you in. Much like the process in the previous awareness steps, we're going to see where else it lives.

I want you to think about all aspects of your life. Here is a list to start with:

- Work life
- Friendships
- Romantic relationships
- Financial
- Family life
- Body image
- Food

Think about things that have happened to you around these specific issues. What has made you feel those exact emotions in your life in each of these areas. How does the same energy live in each area of your life? What are you doing in each of these areas that reinforce the belief that you are holding on to?

The likelihood is your pattern is showing up in all these areas. It is showing up everywhere in your life because you are a walking energetic battery for the pattern. You are the reason why it is alive in your life. When you hold on to the belief and you are the fuel that runs it, then the pattern will continue to be created in all directions.

Since I was dealing feeling with self-worth, here are a few examples of how it showed up for me:

- Work life:
  - I always felt like I should have been paid more for my job.
  - I lost a client today and that made me question my position and if I was doing something wrong.

- Friendships:
  - I wasn't invited to go out with friends.
  - They don't reach out to me as much as they do for our other friends.

- Romantic
  - I don't get touched as much.
  - We never have sex.
  - She doesn't think about me.

- Financial
  - I wish I could go on a vacation.
  - I just had to buy a new fridge.

- We aren't saving.
- My car isn't good enough.
- I can't afford to buy this.

- Body image
  - I am angry because I am balding.
  - I feel unworthy because I don't have a six pack.
  - I can't perform in sports like I want to.
  - I can't lose weight.

- Food
  - I eat junk food and it makes me feel crappy.
  - I can't control my diet because I am emotionally eating.
  - I love sugar because it tastes good.

Your pattern is showing up everywhere. It is a belief built around you and you cannot see anything but this belief. It is like putting on a pair of sunglasses with lenses that restrict your vision. It has imprisoned you and limited you. You are a slave to the belief until you change it.

The flower of life symbol is a graphical depiction of what happens when you imprint a belief in your life. The imprint becomes the center circle of the pattern that every following circle patterns from. It is the core vibration of your trauma. The first circle to be made can be seen outlined in Figure 1.

Figure 1

The next layers of circles are the patterning out of the same energy. It is the outer layer of which the original was laid. The belief or the pattern begins to multiply outward to be experienced in a myriad of ways. Like we have said, the Universe wants to be seen. The Universe will come alive when you place an intention onto something. Each of the outer circles represent an area of your life that the pattern is being seen. It is a shade or a copy of the original circle or imprint. You can see this happening in Figure 2 with the new circles surrounding the original circle.

This patterning out continues outwardly many times over. What you find is an intricate and complex design that looks like the flower of life. The complexities of your life interwoven together when seen from this level. It can be daunting to try to begin your healing, but when you break it down, you find the simplicity of just one circle repeating itself endlessly.

Figure 2

You are becoming aware of the outermost circle that has replicated many times over like the rest of the circles in Figure 3. This is akin to saying there are many layers to an onion. There are many layers to your core imprint, trauma, or pattern. You are only accessing the outermost layer. This exercise is to help you see that there are many circles to the flower or that there are many layers to the onion. There are many shades and colors to self-worth, and you will need to work through each circle to get to the original imprint.

Figure 3

Your pattern is a result of an energetic imprint that you have taken on. It is a belief that has been reinforced within you and you are destined to relive the same pattern repeatedly. In my example, you can see there are many different perspectives to my self-worth. Just like I mentioned in Chapter 2, the law of attraction is at full force here. It will continue to repeat and even get louder until you hear the call.

The Universe is always working for your benefit as the creator, whether it is a negative or positive belief. The law of attraction is going to draw into your reality the exact vibrational match that you are holding on to. It is there to help you confirm and validate your beliefs. It is there to help you see all the different circles you are creating as the creator.

The Universe was confirming my belief about feeling unworthy, and it was reflected everywhere in my reality. Through this exercise, it became apparent that I was creating unconsciously about self-worth issues along with other beliefs as well. It was right in front of my face, and I just could not see it.

Remember that the mind lies to you. It helped you create your beliefs. It helped you become the limited version of you. It is has kept you from seeing the truth about yourself. You cannot always trust your mind. Trust your emotions. Emotions do not lie. In addition to your emotions, your body does not lie. The body is a divine tool for you to use as well. As I said in the previous chapter, the energy comes first, and the physical comes after. The body will provide insight into your patterns.

## Awareness Exercise 4: Body Awareness

Repeat Awareness Exercise 1. This time I want you to pay attention to your body only. Where in your body are you feeling all of this? Where does the energy exists? What chakra do you feel being activated or blocked? Do you feel sluggish? Is there a pain? Does your body lean left or right?

Pay particular attention to any density, sluggishness, or pain in the body. The location of the energy may give insight into what chakra you may have blocks in. When you can establish which chakra is affecting your body, then you can narrow in on what the related issues could be. Go back to Chapter 4 and see what blocks could be impacting you.

For instance, when I go through the exercise, I notice a pain in my lower back. The location of the pain indicates that my root or my sacral chakras are blocked. Using my information about chakras, I can further examine what beliefs I may have around safety or stability within with my materialistic world. Or I could be dealing with some self-confidence issues within my sacral chakra. Perhaps repress emotions or desires that I have not allowed out.

If you find it hard to meditate and want a more concrete process, try the following exercise:

## Writing Exercise 1:

*At the end of the day, write down all the things that made you feel negative emotions. Write down everything that bothered you. Keep the list. Do the same thing for the next day. Write down all the things that bothered you on a new piece of paper. Repeat this every day for a week.*

*When you are done, compare the lists. Compare your experiences from each day and see if there are common themes playing out. There should be a common emotion that is weaving itself throughout the list. This will help you see that a pattern is occurring. Ask yourself, what was happening in those experiences that made you feel these common emotions?*

## Writing Exercise 2:

*Take each aspect of your life. Write down what is going wrong with each area. Or write down what you would like to change in each area. Write down as many things as you can for each aspect of your life.*

*For instance, your work life:*

- *I want to have more money.*
- *I want to be appreciated.*
- *I feel I am overworked.*
- *I feel I should be promoted.*

*Once you are done with each area, compare the lists. There should be a common theme. This should highlight the certain emotions that are occurring in your life.*

# CHAPTER 6:
# START HEALING AND HARMONIZING

**"You are back on track with your destiny."**

**– Spirit Guide**

Healing is not solely a physical recovery. In many ways, the physical symptoms or the physical effects are the results of energy first. Most people focus primarily on the physical and ignore the energetics. It is what we've been taught to focus on. Healing your energetics is just as important as healing your physical and should be treated as such.

When one has a physical wound, it is not in our best interest to continue on with normal life as if nothing happened. It would be in our best interest to rest, tend to the wound, and care for it. One should provide love to the wound so that it may heal quickly. If you ignore it or pretend it is not there, you could reinjure the wound or worsen the original injury. Many of you treat your physical wounds like this. You get a physical wound or an injury and you try to power through it like it does not affect you. Even better, how many of you get sick and act like you are not sick? A sickness overcomes you and you go to work anyways. You act like nothing is wrong and you use your willpower to ride it out. It seems completely ridiculous when you think about it.

How you treat your physical illnesses or physical wounds is a reflection of how you treat yourself. To heal requires you to offer the space for healing. If you break your leg, you need to stop and heal. You cannot force through a broken leg or you could cause irreparable damages. Why is it then, we do not take the same approach when we are dealing with our emotional traumas? There is real pain and damage going on, but many of us just try to avoid it or ignore it. It requires the same healing process as a physical wound. It takes time, attention, and love to heal. We must learn to heal our energetic imprints through self-love and awareness.

My approach to healing is through the awareness of my pains or traumas. Bringing awareness to those rejected aspects of me, providing the much-needed love so that I can heal. This is because you are no longer avoiding something that wants to be seen. You are becoming aware of your energy and aware of your patterns. The awareness of yourself allows you to make changes in the present moment. You are afforded healing by making different choices from your previous traumatized self. You stop the autopilot and start creating new brain synapsis that create new thinking and new patterns.

The healing part of your journey may never fully go away. A friend of mine once said, "Your wounds never go away. They heal, but what is left is a scar." What you have been dealing with is an open wound. When you heal the wound, you will have remnants of it, such as a scar. The pain will be far less, and you will be less energetically charged to it, but there will still be something there. This is to remind you of what you have learned about yourself from the experience. There will be times where you may revisit the scar and understand how it has affected you in other areas.

Think of your life as a spiral. As you become aware of one aspect of yourself, you move through that understanding of yourself. You spend time healing that aspect in a forward progression in your life. Taking time to honor what is there and healing it. The forward progression feels like a movement upward and forward until you bump up against another aspect of the same issue. It will be you in the same place but spiraled to a different view. You are spiraling around to a different awareness about yourself.

This is not a race that you can win. For the more rushed your healing will only increase the resistance for you to move forward. There are no shortcuts. It is only through getting dirty and doing the work with diligence and love will you make your way through. Self-love and healing are not rushed and with haste. It is patience and compassion that one can truly move through into wholeness. You cannot approach your healing in the same manner that got you into the mess.

Your best thinking and actions got you where you are right now. You have used the same thinking, beliefs, and actions to get where you are now. If you are unhappy with your life, then why do you think the same thinking, beliefs, and actions are going to get you somewhere better? You need to change something to get to a different state of being. It is time to stop rejecting yourself. It is time to love yourself.

Let us present ourselves with the pattern in which we would like to change. I recommend utilizing a meditation practice to help silence the mind and bring yourself into center for accessing this information that is unconscious to you. There are many different methods or guided mediations that can help you. I share one method for getting into a meditative state in Chapter 7.

Find a place that you feel comfortable and that you can remain undisturbed for a period. In your meditative state, execute the following steps:

## Step 1: Recall an Experience

Recall the most recent experience that triggered you. This is Awareness Exercise 1 from Chapter 5. Recall an experience that made you feel emotions that are not aligned with what you wanted or that are misaligned emotions. Remember your most recent emotionally triggering experience.

Try to remember everything like you are reliving the situation again and pay attention to the following:

- Your emotions
- What was said to you
- What was done to you
- How it made you feel
- What the environment looked like
- What you were thinking

## Step 2: Initiate a Creator Mindset

Initiate a creator mindset. You must step into the role of the creator and take accountability for your creations. You must become the creator. You must take accountability for what is going wrong in your life. Stepping into the creator mindset is a space of empowerment. It reclaims what you have given away. Becoming the creator automatically removes the victimhood mindset. It puts you into the driver seat and command of the wheel.

Now it is time to inquire into your creations. The first step to becoming aware of your unconscious beliefs is to start asking questions about experiences in your life. When you are emotionally reacting to an external experience, you need to ask about it:

- What am I feeling in the experience?
- What emotions are present?
- What role did I play?
- What role did the co-creator play?
- What was the theme of this interaction?
- Why was this created?
- Why did I create this?
- What lesson is here for me?
- What is driving me to react this way?
- How did this experience come to be?

The creator looks at their experience like a child exploring their world. A child seeks to understand how things come to be with an open and exciting mindset. Be like the child in wonderment of your world. Seek deeply to know your reality and creation.

Continue to inquire and deeply understand the entire experience. Thoroughly seek to find the underlying energy that is trying to communicate with you. Look beyond the surface. Seek to find the why. Try to uncover that aspect of you that was rejected.

The law of attraction is always working. In this misaligned creation, the law of attraction is still at work and working correctly. It does not subjectively choose which things bring to you. You are being showed something about yourself through this experience. It must be so. Whether you wanted it or not, it came to be. Therefore, the mirror is reflecting it to you.

In most cases, you are being reflected an emotion. I previously stated that you must be honest with yourself. Sometimes that can be difficult and that is why it is important to focus on your emotions. This is because your emotions do not lie. Your emotions are the true north on the compass. They will lead you toward your hidden traumas and patterns. Try to understand why you are having these emotions and feel them.

When you can understand your emotions, you can work back to when you first felt them. You are looking for the original imprint of the pattern. You are looking for the energy you did not express.

Do not forget about the body here. Try to feel where it is held in the body. Do you hold it in your gut, your legs, your arms, neck, back, etc.? Ask it to step forward and share information with you:

- When were you created?
- Why are you there?
- What are you trying to tell me?
- What emotion do you hold?

It is vitally important to allow yourself to feel your emotions here. To really sit with all that has been buried. If you get an emotional outpouring at this stage, then you need to sit in the energy and truly feel all that is there. Let yourself feel these things as opposed to repressing them. When you feel that you have allowed it to be felt and all the energy to come up and out, then you can move on. I remember when I was working on this regarding my mother. I had a lot of guilt, shame, and pain from our relationship. I began to cry uncontrollably the minute I started to think about it. My head wanted to fall into my chest, and I felt so sad. I repeated this many times. I kept sitting in that energy until it was honored, and I did not have the same emotional and physical response as before.

What you are trying to achieve through this step is honoring the emotions or energies that were repressed in the experiences. We are trying to bring balance to these energies that have been denied. In a sense, we are trying to love what we have rejected about ourselves. This helps heal the divine feminine energies. As we mentioned, we are neglecting the other half of us. The divine feminine is what we create from. We must rebalance. We are neutralizing the energy to become whole and still.

As a creator, you are creating or manifesting with the divine feminine energy. Right now, the divine energy is not balanced. The potentials from which you create from, which is the divine feminine energy, are based on judgements, biases, and fears. The imbalances within your divine energies imprint into your creation because you are using imbalanced energies. As you move about and create with the divine masculine energy you get reflections of the imbalances. By bringing awareness to ourselves and inquiring about our patterns we allow these things to come to the surface and be brought back to neutral. We allow ourselves to have a balance potential that we can use to create with the divine masculine.

It is important to understand that you may not get any answers right away. Just be patient. Trust that your body will release the information to you and trust that you will come to understand it. It will most likely come to you as a memory or just as a feeling. This may also take several times before you can access the information. There could be may reasons for why you may not get an answer. The main reason is that you may not be ready to see it. When you are, it will be revealed to you at the right time.

I remember when I was writing this book, I came to a point where I did not know how to move forward. I was stuck on how to get an editor or how to move through the editing process. I did not know who to trust and where to go. I was thinking about all sorts of different ways and was constantly looking for guidance. During this time, I developed an acute injury to my ankle and knee. The pain was intense enough that I had trouble walking. Going up and down the stairs took longer because I had to climb one step at a time while holding on to the railing. I thought perhaps it was from running. I meditated and thought about the energy and the pain in my knee for the next couple of days, asking "What is this about?" "Why can't I move?" "What is causing me to feel stuck?" The answer did not come to me. I was open to hearing and getting the answer, but it just was not time for me to know.

A couple of days later I had a call with a publisher. The call answered many of my questions, especially around the editing process. I got clarity on what editors to trust and what I needed to do. Right after the call, the pain in my ankle and knee started to clear. I was able to walk better and go up and down the stairs, whereas that morning I was unable to put weight on my right leg. A few hours later, it was completely gone. I was shocked and realized what the energy was all about. It revealed itself to me when the time was right and I was ready to understand it.

## Step 3: Be Grateful and Forgive

When you are in the creator mindset, there is gratitude for your creations. It is by your hand and desire that your experience came to be. Revel in the magic that is your power. There must be gratitude for what you made. It is by your own creative intent that the law of attraction brought your experience to your doorstep. Your energy and your vibrational being are what brought your reality into existence. You are the reason why you are where you are now. Be grateful for that power.

If not, you are in a state of resistance. You are saying that I am rejecting what is happening and I will not take any accountability for it. This is a state of disempowerment and victimhood. This is denying yourself, denying your own energy, and denying your divinity. You are rejecting what you are. That is exactly why you are dealing with your pattern. Resistance is like swimming against a strong current in a river. You are fighting the flow; you are expending all your energy to fight it and it will exhaust you.

Gratitude is grace. Gratitude is going with the flow of the Universe because it is acceptance. You are in acceptance of life without judgement. You are accepting your creations in the moment rather than being in resistance. Gratitude helps you remain neutral to the experience. It helps you move through rather than hold on to. Be grateful for what is happening now and allow it to flow through and out. For gratitude is swimming with the current of the river and you expend little energy floating with the river.

Within the space of gratitude, you can offer forgiveness to yourself and co-creators. Forgiving has many healing properties. Without forgiveness you cannot let go of the energy that you took on. You cannot remove the density of the traumas that have occurred and stuck within your energy field. Forgiveness is more about you than it is about the other.

What does it mean to forgive? Much like the state of gratitude, to forgive is to let go. It is to allow energy to move on. This includes all parties. You no longer hold on to grudges that keep you in the same pattern. It allows the other to be freed from the energy you hold against them. It is acceptance and releasing.

My perspective on forgiveness is based on the oneness that we seek. It is related to your awareness as the creator. As a creator, you are aware of your creations. You are aware you are creating or co-creating with another creator to help you see more about yourself. It is much easier to expand on experiences and understanding of self when you have someone else play the roles for you. To experience what it is like to be a victim, you need a perpetrator to cause you pain. To feel what it is like to be betrayed, you require someone to betray you. To experience and understand love, you need someone to love. This awareness allows you to see the experience from another perspective. It allows you to see how the pieces of this life experience were brought into your reality without judgement. It allows you to understand the vibrations at play. The creator sees that each co-creator helped you understand your hurt, pain, suffering, etc. The creator understands the match to their vibration or life intentions.

These co-creators helped you see something about yourself. You magnetize the co-creator into your reality to play a role for you to help you understand yourself. These co-creators are perfect divine beings matching to your vibration to express the vibrational energy you are holding. It was but only through your own intention and energy that you brought about this co-creation. Therefore, forgiveness is needed to allow the co-creator to move on. Forgiveness is needed to all for you to move on.

Forgiveness is the claiming of that which you have given away. It is through the outside world that you have given your power to. The power to have a joyous and loving life is given to another. Do you really want someone else to dictate how you feel at any given moment? Forgiveness allows you to say, "No more will I allow myself to be dictated by past events! No longer shall I let my future be dictated by someone! I claim my happiness, I claim my love, and I claim my power!" Forgiveness allows you to move forward in life.

Forgiveness allows you to finally release the burden of the energy. As you know, when you hold on to anger, hurt, hatred, and sadness the emotional body can't express it in a healthy way and it becomes part of your field. Like a seed, the energy becomes part of your field and grows outwardly, expanding itself through the flowering of the patterns that make up your life today. Your patterns are but the infinite patterns of the same emotional trauma, the same energetic seed from that moment. What you see is the blooming of flowers springing forth from the same energy that is your reality playing out in a myriad of ways. Forgiveness is the step needed to start integrating the energy and transmuting it for your highest good. Forgiveness releases you from the trapped trauma that keeps you stuck.

Again, this is continuing the process of balancing out the divine feminine energies you are creating with. Grace is within the acceptance, gratitude, and forgiveness. These help with honoring what is and neutralizing the creative energy within you.

## Step 4: Feel What You Want to Feel

We experience a negative emotion when there is a disconnect between what we want and what we experience. You are feeling the dissonance of your creations. The negative emotions are the feedback from it. When we do not honor it in the moment, we are left with an energy imbalance within us. We must try to figure out how to rebalance the energy. The previous step was to help find what that emotional imbalance was. The next step is to rebalance it.

Now that you understand what your emotional imbalance or wound is, we can change it. In most cases what you wanted to feel in that memory was love and acceptance. You wanted to receive the opposite of what you experienced. You wanted to feel loved in that moment. There are many different shades of love. It could be validation, support, happiness, abundance, freedom, etc., but when you boil it down, we are mostly dealing with love.

Take this time to imagine and feel what it would be like to get what you wanted from the experience. Feel what you needed at that time. Truly embody the feeling of what it would feel like to have been loved instead of the trigger or reliving the trauma. Embodiment of this energy is different than just thinking about it. What you are trying to experience is the act of being loved. How does being squeezed tightly from a hug feel? How does your energy feel when you are hugged, loved, and accepted? Feel it as if it were real and happening to you. As if you truly believe that you are loved.

The easiest way is to feel love is to remember the last time you felt it. Try to remember the experience and the sensations. Try to relive it and embody it. Feel what it was like through your entire energy system. Bring it all up and be in that space. Once you can recall the memory and the feeling, you can offer yourself the same feeling in another memory. You can offer yourself love energy whenever you want. It is now a tool for you to use. A great vibrational state of being that you have access to whenever you desire.

Your entire energy field cannot tell the different between the past and now. Your body and your energy do not know the difference between what happens in your memory and now. You cannot tell the difference between pain that occurred five to ten years ago or that which was five seconds ago. This is because there is only the current moment. You can experience what you wanted to feel in the past even though you are working on your energy in the present moment. This allows you to change the entire energetic of that memory which changes your energy that you hold currently in the now moment.

That tells you that time is irrelevant to the healing process. What you are doing is basically imprinting a new energy where the old energy was. You are replacing it with something that you wanted to feel instead. Take your time. Take as long as you need to feel loved. Recall anything that makes you feel supported, validated, and loved. Anything that you need to help you feel what you wanted to feel rather than what you did feel. If you do not have a memory with loving feelings, make it up. Like is said, your energy is just as receptive to imagination as it is to real life experience. Imagine what it would be like to have someone hug you, smother you in kisses, and tell you how much you are loved (you would laugh at this if you could actually see the amount of loving and supportive spirits you have around you at any given time). I have done this for myself many times. All that matters is you get to the space where you feel loved.

I remember I was dealing with a memory where I was being beat by my father with a belt. I had all this fear and pain in me. I felt so unloved, rejected, and scared. In this step of the process, I changed the memory. I felt what I wanted to feel. I wanted to feel loved and safe. I became the source of that for myself. I envisioned an older version of myself stopping my father from hitting me with the belt. I saw myself stop his hand from swinging and pushed him out. I watched myself come to me and give me the biggest hug of love and compassion. I told myself what I wanted to hear, that I am safe and loved. I felt that energy within my whole being. I remained in that space as long as I wanted and until it no longer needed attention.

At this step, we have neutralized the previous charge in your divine feminine energies. We have brought the divine feminine into wholeness by removing the judgements and biases within your creative energies. This makes the potentials of your life open up again because we cleared out the limited beliefs and rejected energies associated with this experience.

What you are doing here is generating new divine feminine energies that are based in love rather than fear. You are embodying the divine feminine energies of connection, peace, and love throughout your entire energy field. It is like you are creating an energy portal within. A portal for you to walk through to all the potentials that match what you desire.

You are creating a different stream of energy compared to before. This time with far more power of Source love from which to magnetize from. The Universe will respond to that energy as you swirl that throughout your energy field.

## Step 5: Draw the Energy into the Now Moment

Once you feel what you wanted to feel in the memory, draw the energy into the now moment. Bring the energy into your life now. How? By being grateful for the things in your life that provide the same feeling you just offered to yourself. Be grateful for the experiences in your life that currently offer you love, joy, happiness, etc. Find something in your life that offers that exact vibration that you felt in Step 4. Think about things in your life that can offer the same energy. Open your perspective to the many things that can be found in the moment that offer you what you want to feel.

The limited lenses we have on do not allow us to see certain things even though they are right under our noses. When you can hold the space and energy of what you want to feel, it allows you to see beyond the lenses that you have been wearing. Your field of vision opens up and you can see more clearly or see what was hiding. Utilizing gratitude with the energies you are feeling, you can shift your perspective about things that are happening in your life. You can open up to the joy, love, and abundance that has been there all along. Things that are simple but you have taken for granted.

Take my previous example in Step 4. After providing myself love and being in that space, I then thought about my life now. I brought up experiences that matched the same love and safety I felt. I was grateful for sitting in the sun and feeling the warmth on my body. I was grateful that my daughter gave me a hug and said, "I love you, Daddy." I was grateful for the love and support of my guides. There are infinite things to be grateful for in the now moment. Capitalize on the energy of what you are feeling and bring gratitude for what you have in your life now that offers the same energy. Be grateful for it now.

This step is harnessing the divine feminine energies that you have created within yourself. It is bringing the new loving embodiment into the current now moment. In the previous step, it was like you opened an energy portal to this state of being. Now it is like you have just gone through it and are finding the vibrational energy. It is like you passed through the doorway and can see into the new world that is based in Source love. You open your eyes, and you see things that were never seen before. You see things that are much different. You have become the state of being that you desired, right now in your life. It is a new world.

## Step 6: Repeat Steps 1-5 (if time allows)

Recall Awareness Exercise 3 from Chapter 5. If you are afforded the time, repeat the same process again but with another memory that contains the exact vibrational energy as the one you just healed through. Think about all the aspects of your life impacted by this vibration. Try to find where else this energy is playing out and revisit those memories the best that you can. You are essentially spiraling back through your memories toward the original imprint. Healing each circle of your flower of life pattern as you move toward the center circle. You are clearing each outer circle and moving inward. You are recollecting lost pieces of yourself at every circle until you reach the original trauma itself where you will be whole again.

## Step 7: Take Action with the Energy

Once you are ready to move forward, it is time to harness that energy. Take all the love that you have embodied in yourself with in Steps 4 and 5 and act upon it. Action is thought or energy in motion. Since you are now in a state of being of love and gratitude, seed the next now moment with that energy. Go do something with that energy. Take action! Action signals to the Universe that you are moving with a vibrational intention embodied with what you want, and it will respond to it.

Many people will just sit and daydream all day and wonder why it does not work. It does not work because there is no action. You must harness the divine feminine energy you have just experienced by taking action with the divine masculine energy. Manifest more experiences by taking action with it. Create with the energy you just created within you. The law of attraction has but to answer the call and magnetize those experiences. The new energy can start patterning out. Create through action the new higher vibration of love.

If you truly wanted something in your life, you would do whatever you could to attain it. Think about the simple process of going to buy a stick of gum. You desire a piece of gum. You think about chewing gum and how it would taste. This inspires you and you decide to take action. You fully embodied the energy of chewing gum. You get into your car and drive to the store. You get out of the car and walk into the store and purchase the stick of gum. Thus, completing what you desire and becoming the state of being of happily chewing your gum.

This is a simple example of taking action with full embodiment of aligned energy. To achieve the state of being of chewing gum, the full embodiment of accomplishing your goals, required all the actions aligned with getting that gum. It shows you that it means you have to fully embody what a person would do to accomplish their desires. You must do what someone would do to achieve the states of being that they want. It does not come with just one or two steps. It comes will fully acting out what it takes. The action step toward what you want is but one step. What other things are required of you to become that state of being you desire? You must become it and take action as if you are living it.

This step is about harnessing the divine masculine energies. You can now use the divine masculine energies in a balanced approach with the divine feminine energies. You are fully embodied with the full potential of Source love energy. The infinite abundance is within you now to create from as the creator.

The creator can now take action to build in alignment with all that is coursing through you. This time in a space and embodiment that is not about rejection, separation, and fear. It is now in the space of the empowered creator who is loved and more peaceful. Use the creative force that is the divine masculine and act.

You have walked through the portal and are now adventuring around the new world. Be in wonder, be in excitement as you build through the new you. Continue to act with that energy. Become the creator in this new world.

## Step 8: Practice and Stay Aware

This is the part that we all tend to have difficulty with. It takes practice to move from unaware, unconscious living to a state of more awareness. It takes time to remain aware of yourself. Practice and diligence to remain present with your life and to notice when things are occurring and to not fall into old, recreated patterns. It can be easy to get trapped in the downward spiral of your energetic triggers if you do not remain diligent. This is not an overnight event nor a quick one at that. It took me thirty plus years to become aware that I needed to change. It will take some time to unravel those years of experiences.

It is a process that is never ending. It is a mountain that never ends. It does not mean that the climb is always steep and treacherous. There will be easier parts of the trail and your journey, but there will be times where you will be tested. That is all that life is, a process of ebb and flow to know yourself through the limitations that are your life.

The key here is not to recreate the same pattern. I say recreate rather than react for two reasons: 1) You are not a victim and 2) you are the creator. You are the one creating. The creator mindset removes the victimhood mindset. You are accountable, so own it. How can you be a victim of your own creations? It may certainly feel that way, but I assure you it is not. As a creator, you are always creating. What we want to do is not recreate the same pattern but create something new. If you are recreating the experiences, that means they must serve you for a reason. Just remember as you move through your journey, you will undoubtably revisit these things again.

When faced with a triggering experience that is reflecting your old patterns, it is vital that you do not behave and respond as you have always done. This is because your old pattern is on auto pilot. It needs to be taken off. You need to stop the printing press that you have unconsciously been creating from.

Awareness and the mere idea of being present in any situation creates something new. It breaks the unconscious patterns that you have always followed. By becoming the creator and being aware through your day, you change your energy. You change who you are. This allows you to not follow with the old synapsis created in your brain; you are creating new synapsis to behave differently.

Taking an action step in a triggered emotional state will continue to seed the next moment with that energy. Have you ever noticed the chaos that can ensue when you are constantly running around angry and triggered? So, by creating a different action, a different behavior, you are seeding the next moment with a different energy. You will be seeding the next moment in a more neutral state. One that is more centered and energized with self-love.

A moment of clarity should be made here. I must emphasize again that this is a process and it takes practice. There are many different shades to the energy that you are holding on to. It has patterned out in your life in a myriad of ways. You are becoming aware of your patterns and this level of awareness is perhaps just the first layer of the metaphoric onion. Much like the Awareness

Exercise 3 you did in Chapter 5, you can see how it plays out everywhere. You will continue to revisit your repressed energies over and over again because they are deeply intertwined within. In addition, you may think that you have cleared and healed a trauma, only to find at some later point that you are dealing with the exact same thing. This is not a failure on your part or that you did something wrong. It is merely a chance to honor what is being brought up and to offer a deeper love than what was given previously. Think of it as a deeper cleaning to make sure that all the grime and old dirt comes out.

I am not trying to make you feel defeated but to encourage you. You are not failing. You are indeed succeeding anytime you choose to love yourself. The act of self-love is never a failure. When the energy is most palpable and most difficult is typically when we feel defeated. This is true when you seem to revisit the same pattern again. This may seem like a failure, but in fact the opposite is most likely. You are succeeding in your growth. As we discussed in the previous chapter with the flower of life symbol, you are breaking through one circle into the next circle. You are peeling the onion back to another level. You are indeed spiraling to the same thing but at a different level. It is the last catalyst of seeing all there is to that circle before you see the next. You are about to move into the next circles of your illusion. See Figure 4.

Figure 4

This journey of becoming the creator is constant and akin to a never-ending journey up the mountain. There will be days you feel like you are stumbling or feel like you are tumbling backwards. There will be days that it may take everything you've got to go one inch. In those times, I assure you that progress is being made. At each step and at each effort to improve is a movement forward. What you will find though, is at certain points in your journey you can look around and notice how much better your life is.

You are right where you need to be. You are perfect where you are, right now. There is a lot of truth to that statement. I say that because many of you will often try to rush your healing and become inpatient. You may feel like you have plateaued and get frustrated with your meditations or not being able to break through your patterns. I assure you things are progressing, but there will be many times where you do not know what you do not know. There is a misunderstanding of the magnitude to your healing, and you are not ready to peel that layer back. You may even say, "I am ready! I want this to change now." Yet, the answer does not come right away. Do not despair, dear ones. These moments are typically a benefit for you. Ones that you may not be able to understand at the moment, but are most beneficial for you. From my experience, it typically means that you are not quite ready to uncover a truth or disrupt your illusions. For if the answers or the awareness come too quickly and powerfully, you could have immense difficulty transcending them. It would be the wrong place at the wrong time.

These liminal spaces that you will find yourself in are a gift of preparedness. For preparedness will be warranted as the call outward for healing is heard and Source begins to respond. It is my experience that a floodgate opens when the creator is ready to see. When you are ready, a cascade of emotions come through as you rapidly spiral through your repressed energies. It takes a great test of self to remain aware through this pivotal point. Those that are not ready will not heal but recreate and repeat their traumas. They will fall back into the patterns they so desperately seek to get out of. It is the Universe testing you if you are ready to take more on and some do not pass.

Daily Exercise for Awareness Check-In:

*Set an alarm for every couple of hours. At each alarm, check in with yourself and ask the following questions:*

1. *How am I feeling right now?*

2. *What does my body feel like?*
3. *Where in my body do I feel dis-ease?*
4. *What beliefs do I hold about myself in the moment?*
5. *What beliefs do I hold about what I am experiencing?*
6. *Am I in fear? Or am I in love?*
7. *If it is fear, then what are you fearing?*

*Sit with what you observe. If you are experiencing any misaligned energies, then take the opportunity to honor the energy being presented in the moment. Inquire about it because it is the unconscious programs that are popping up.*

Our experiences are divine and purposeful. They are there for a reason. We code them as negative or positive, or good or bad. We desire to shed the negative experiences and throw them aside. In the end, that was just like us repressing the energies in the first place. As great as that would be, to cut them out and remove them, how would that serve you and your greater expansion if you could basically remove them completely? You would not be able to understand yourself as Source if you were to be able to say, "No, thank you. I'll leave this here," or "I don't like how I feel, so I will focus on this feeling." It is through the process of becoming the creator and loving what you have made that brings healing. We should not reject what has happened to us just because it was hurtful. It was divine in some sense. Remember, you chose to experience this before you incarnated into this life.

What I found with my own process is that patterns repeat themselves no matter how many times that I try to move beyond my hurt and traumas by saying, "I don't need this anymore." (That on its own level is avoidance, which is still holding on to the energy.) The pattern always found a way back into my experience. I would find myself always asking, "Why? Why after recognizing the feeling and releasing it, does it keep coming back?" As long as you maintain the energy within yourself and remain unconscious of it, it will repeat in your life. As much as I prefer not to have redundancy, this requires repeating. As long as you hold on to the energy and remain unconscious of it, it will repeat in your life. The experience may not be the same, but the energetic and emotional representation will be exact.

Now, I am not discounting the process of remaining positive. I believe it to be a useful tool. The truth of the matter is if you are reading this book then chances are you are not of an awareness required to holding the intention of positivity to manifest positive experiences in your life. Here is an exercise: Try to remain conscious of how you feel emotionally, physically, energetically, and mentally for more than ten minutes within your day. How did it go? Likely, you are probably thrown off by an external event and your focus goes elsewhere. Your unconscious mind and ego are likely running the show the majority of your awake time. Since you are mostly running unconscious through the day, they are going to manifest the things you are holding on to unconsciously.

It is an integration of a paradox. As you become more aware of yourself, you will find being positive comes naturally. It is the openness of Source connection that allows you to see more love in your life. You do not need to focus on being positive. It should not have to come with a great amount of energy. Being positive should come naturally.

Forcing a positive mindset is resistance to what is happening in your life. It is usually a sign that one is avoiding an aspect of themselves. Forcing positivity is rejecting the divine feminine energies and using the mental divine masculine energies to create results. This will only create further imbalanced energies from which we create from and cause the same experiences we are trying to fix to perpetuate.

It is the integration of the trauma and the awareness of the trauma that allows you to move beyond it. This allows for the full expression of Source through you to move forward. The full expression of Source energy through you, is the healing. When one does not allow that true expression of divine Source energy to be expressed, then the imprint is made. It is in that moment you have held on to the expression of that energy and created an energetic magnetism. How do you become aware? You must revisit the trauma or the pain in the NOW moment. You must relive it and allow the expression of the imprint. You must allow Source energy to be expressed in all its love. Then you can become aware of it, and you can remain conscious of it.

## DARK NIGHT OF THE SOUL

I feel compelled at this point to help you understand a spiritual concept that is deeply impactful. You will undoubtably come into a place that many on the spiritual path would call the dark night of the soul. It is important to understand this concept as you begin to heal and understand yourself. There will be a time when all that you have known and identified with will all come crashing down and cease to serve you. It is at this precious time that many seekers of truth and healing will be tested by the removing of their false garments, if you will.

So, what is the dark night of the soul? One definition is the desolation, the isolation, the disconnect in which one may experience as separation from the divine. My experience of this is the experience in which the creator is stripped bare of what they have known in this earthly plane. This leads to a variable degree of discomfort for the creator, depending on the level of attachment to their false identities.

7 signs:

1. You feel a deep sense of sadness, which often verges on despair. (This sadness is often triggered by the state of your life, humanity, and/or the world as a whole.)
2. You feel an acute sense of unworthiness.
3. You have the constant feeling of being lost or "condemned" to a life of suffering or emptiness.
4. You possess a painful feeling of powerlessness and hopelessness.
5. Your will and self-control are weakened, making it difficult for you to act.
6. You lack interest and find no joy in things that once excited you.
7. You crave for the loss of something intangible; a longing for a distant place or to "return home" again.

Many will experience this, especially as we move through this period of transition. We will likely be forced into confronting our egos and that which is our higher self. How much of it are you willing to let go? How attached are you to things that do not serve you? How willing are you to dive into the darkness of yourself to emerge reconnected with the true piece of you? You must go through a death of your projected identities that you have placed value and power onto. This is the dark night of the soul, but on the other end is the light. At the end of the night comes a new day. A light that shines brightly. The bright light is you, knowing yourself. You will become more than you have ever known yourself to be even though you shed so much from your life.

## Limited on Time? Need a Quick Fix?

*We all have had those moments where we come into an experience that is flipping the switch on your traumas. They usually come at the most inconvenient times, and we cannot afford the time to go through the whole process outlined above. We can start the negative spiral and start drawing in the worst-case scenarios if we do not change our energy. Sometimes we need a quick shift of energy to help out until we can sit and dedicate more time to self-love. Try this:*

*When you can, stop for a minute and close your eyes. Draw into your now moment a memory that holds what you want to feel. Something that feels good. Relive it like it is happening now in your head. Then open your eyes and keep that energy in your energy field. Take an action step with the energy to create the next now moment in your life. Seed the next moment with the way you want to feel.*

*More times than naught, this little quick fix can shift the energy to not manifest the worst-case scenarios. You are basically interjecting on a vibrational pattern and moving into a different pattern.*

# CHAPTER 7:
# FINDING YOUR TRUTH

The spiritual path is never ending. You can always find out more about yourself through the infinite ways of the Universe. The path which you take will feel like you are on a hike up an endless mountain. I say endless because there is no end to Source. How can there be an end to infinity? Source is infinite. As you begin your journey, you find yourself with infinite trails and walkways to start on. All you understand is there are views to be had and it is an upward trajectory that you must embark on. Throughout your hike you continue to see many parallel paths but just slightly different than yours. Some zig while yours zag. Some loop around and some move straight upward. Each path taking its own way, but overall they are all heading up the mountain.

Sometimes the paths lead to a common place and sometimes they do not. Some paths have a little clearing for you to rest and reflect. A clearing among the trails to gaze outwardly at the beauty. A place in the journey where you can look out and see your progress. You can see the landscape. You can see how far you have come. There will be beauty in each step of your journey.

Not all parts of your journey will feel like you are progressing in a steady incline to better views. There will be parts of your journey that feel like you are not making progress or are even falling behind. There will be easy terrain to traverse like valleys or gullies. There will be extremely difficult terrain to traverse like rocky cliffs or steep and narrow areas. There will be times where you think you are slipping and taking two steps backwards, or even falling back completely.

It is an endless, beautiful, upward journey. There will be days that will feel more difficult than others. Some days you may not want to walk any further. I assure you there will be days you wish not to climb at all and give up. Rest assured, as long as you make steps then there is progress. It may not feel like it, but each step is progress. It still is progress even though it may feel like you have taken two steps backwards. Each time you do that, the view of the upward will get better. At another clearing in your journey, you will look back and say how wonderful each step was and see the wisdom of it all.

Diamonds are made from coal. It is through constant environmental changes, shifts, pressure, and heat that coal can become a diamond over time. Your human existence is part of that process. For the essence that makes up you, the soul or the spark that is Source, is refining itself through life lessons. It is fulfilling its spiritual desires about itself. Your experience as human, in a sense, is a microcosm of that process. Under great pressures will you ultimately learn the deep love that is you. You will become stronger and more loving and compassionate than ever before. Through the unimaginable trials and troubles that your path may lead you, they are all designed to help you overcome something or to help you become something better. To crystalize you into the diamond.

The spiritual healing path is finding the truth about yourself. You will undoubtedly venture into many different areas that help you further your spiritual growth and seek your own truth. There are many ways humanity has tried to create connection to Source. Many ways humanity tries to find its way back to oneness. Think about all the different practices out there that provide paths to universal love and feeling Source connection. There are numerous yoga practices, mediating, chanting, ayahuasca or other psychedelic drugs, etc. The list goes on. All of these human creations, variations of practices, are to briefly feel what has always been within. The important thing to remember is, whatever path you take, do what feels right for you. Do what is resonating with your being.

What I care to share with you at this juncture of our journey are a few practices or additional tools to help you on your journey. Tools and practices that have helped me with my own journey in self-discovery. My truths that could help you with your truth. That means you need a sense of discernment. Discernment is key as you move forward in your life. For there are many truths, many paths, and many pitfalls that can distract you. You need a way to tell what true north for you is. Here is a little exercise to help you find your true north on your compass. A template to gauge what is right for you.

### Truth Exercise:

*Say your full name out loud. As you do it, notice there are no hesitations. Notice how it feels within your body. Notices how saying your name does not cause any energetic dissonance. There is flow and alignment. It is truth.*

*Now say out loud a different name that is not yours.*

*"I AM _____!"*

*Whatever name you chose to say, notice the energetic difference. Let us imagine you said, "I AM JOHN DOE." There should be a noticeable difference between saying "JOHN DOE" compared to your actual name. What are your reactions? Can you say it with a straight face? Was there hesitation in your voice? How did the energy feel? Did you laugh? Did you cringe? Did one of you chakras act differently?*

*This is a thermometer for what is true for you. It is how you can gauge how the energy flows within you. It is your temperature test to know if things resonate with you or not. If what you say or hear resonates with you, then it might be something to explore. If it does not resonate, then perhaps it is something to avoid or mull over for a bit until you find out more information. Notice that I say, "true for you." I did not say it is "THE TRUTH." It is only "a" truth for the moment. For there are many truths and many truths can exist at the same time. The Source holds infinite truths, and you will undoubtably come across many truths during your journey. This exercise can be expanded further out to all aspects of your life.*

## MEDITATION

If there is one practice that has change my life completely, it has been meditation. Mediation has been instrumental to my vibrational awareness and spiritual life. The meditative state has been my doorway to healing my traumas and remembering my connection with Source. It has allowed me to rediscover parts of me that were given away to fear and to reclaim myself as sovereign.

Many of us are too busy with life and the different roles that we play. Sometimes we are just too busy to digest our emotions in depth on the fly. You need a time, a space holder to unravel the feedback that are your emotions. Without mediation, we can miss the great opportunities to inquire about our experiences. We would miss the ability to inquire triggering events if we did not have time for meditation. Meditation allowed me to feel my emotions. It allowed me to see why I was holding on to so much anger. Without meditation, I would not be where I am today, and I would not have opened up to spirit.

I believe a meditative practice is a foundation to your own spiritual and healing path. I encourage you to meditate with an enormous amount of gusto because of how transformation I believe it to be. There is no better time to start than now. In addition, there is not a right or wrong way of doing it. There are many different meditation methods that include breathing techniques and guides. What is important is that you start and over time you will find what works best for you.

There are several reasons for mediation:

- Helps illuminate areas that you are studying
- Provides insight into problems you are dealing with
- Inspiration for new creativity or innovation
- Provides momentary oneness with Source
- Insight into the law of nature
- Recalibrate your energy field

I recommend finding a quiet place to meditate. I grew up in an education system that had an open concept structure. We had classrooms in large cubicles. There were only dividers between classes. You could see people walking by because there were no doors. You can hear all the different teachers talking and their students in one space. It was extremely difficult to focus. So, find yourself a quiet place where you can be removed from distractions.

I recommend sitting on a comfortable chair or in a cross-legged position. I prefer to have my spinal column upright rather than horizontal. For me, in a meditative position such as laying on my back, it can be difficult to stay awake.

Take several deep clearing breaths, in through the nose and out through the mouth. Try to get the inhales to reach down into your stomach. The reason for this is to calm your vagus nerve. The vagus nerve runs nearly the length of your body. It stimulates the fight or flight response within you. Deep breathing into your stomach can help calm this response and help you feel safer in your body.

After several clearing breaths, settle into your normal breathing pattern. Think about the infinity sign in the sense of continuation of inhaling and exhaling without stopping. As you do, place your attention on your breath. Watch it enter and leave your body. This will help you focus your mind.

Some of you may experience what I call "monkey brain." Imagine a monkey jumping around in a cage and acting out by throwing bananas. Much like the monkey jumping around and getting your attention, you may have constant thoughts that pop in from nowhere. The constant chatter of the mind and the thoughts that seem to pop in from nowhere. If this happens, just draw your awareness back to your breath. Focus on the breath again and allow your thoughts to float by. If need be, go back to the clearing breaths.

I recommend starting out with five to ten minutes of mediation. As you become more proficient, you can increase the time in meditation. When you feel proficient enough, you can utilize the time in mediation to achieve the results mentioned above. This is especially powerful when working through the healing process of your traumatic memories.

## BODY MOVEMENT

You are here physically. You chose to be here in the physical. Whether you like it or not, you are here for a reason. You did not incarnate here just to spend your entire time trying to get out of your body. There is nowhere to go and there is nowhere to be, but right here and now. So, get used to being in the body. This means your physical presence is part of your divine experience to know yourself. You are learning what it is like to be Source in a material existence. The physical aspect of you is divine and we must honor that as well.

Sometimes our experiences can certainly feel unbearable and hard. It can be almost impossible to understand why we experience things here. There are things that may not resonate with you, and you tend to be less present in the moment. That leads many of you to try to leave your body. You are constantly outside of your body and not being present with yourself. When many of you feel the external pressures of life, feel externally threatened or fearful your energy leaves the present moment. You feel fear and out you go, away from your body and the moment. You are spending energy outside your body. You wander off into in the future or the past, and completely ignore the present moment which holds your physical body.

I remember a message from a spirit around this topic. I was having a discussion with a spirit at a table. There was a gathering of people and a table with an empty seat. I made the choice to come to the gathering and to sit down. When I sat down at the table, a spirit asked me to leave. I remember feeling like I was about to accept that request but changed my mind. I replied, "No, I will not leave. I decided to come here, and I will stay here. I decided to come here whether I like it or not. Being in the body is important and I will stay and honor that." At that point, the spirit nodded, and I telepathically understood the reason for our conversation.

We are spending a lot of our experience outside the body. It is important to get comfortable with our bodily existence. This is a process and practice, and it does not change overnight. The practice becomes easier as you move through your spiritual and healing journey. This is because your body is part of that self-discovery journey. Being present and safe within the body will become more natural as you increase your awareness.

I highly recommend something to move the body. For many people, their mind is mostly fixated on the physical. Seeing the physical is confirmation or validation for their beliefs. As much as I discuss the energetics, the physical is important as well. Doing something that gets the body moving will help force some of the energetics to move. So, I recommend getting out and exercising. Any exercise is good.

There is no disagreement to the benefits of getting outside and exercising. Open up the lungs and breathe, which helps detox. The blood flow picks up and brings oxygen to the cells. Your brain releases endorphins, you sleep better, you start to burn excess sugars, and your liver can detox better. There are numerous benefits to exercise; everything benefits from it. It helps you emotionally, mentally, energetically, and physically. If your energetics are all in alignment, then your physical body will follow suit.

Exercise is a great alchemical process. As we all know, when we are feeling certain emotions, physical exercise can help us move that emotion. For instance, getting angry at a situation, we can choose to redirect that anger into something more constructive. Go for a run, the exerting of energy through the heat of exercise can burn or alchemize the emotion. Note of caution: Be careful not to use this as an avoidance mechanism so that you do not need to confront your traumas. It is one thing to want to exercise to help work through something, but it is another thing when you use it to classically avoid your emotions.

I have great appreciation for Kundalini yoga. An old friend and beautiful soul recommended it several times before I decided to overcome my inertia and do it. Like I have mentioned, the body will hold energy and most times it can be unconscious energy. The experience of Kundalini yoga, or any yoga not aforementioned, is a great opportunity to release it. Kundalini yoga is a mind, body, and spirit experience to raise your vibration or awareness of self. Utilizing sound, body movement, and breathing techniques can help you really move your body around and transmute stagnant stale energy.

Whatever physical practice you chose, be mindful that physical intention will manifest energies to be integrated. What I mean is when you look to work on yourself physically, the energy must also adjust too. Focusing on the physical will force the dormant or repressed energy out of the body. You will be confronted by it in a visceral way. The energy must be cleared out as well to allow something new in. Something must go before you can shift, otherwise you will experience everything you were trying to avoid.

I remember a time when my wife was trying to feel better about herself. She wanted to look better and be healthier rather than feel like a failure. So, she decided to go on a juice cleanse. She focused the healing on the physical without any attention to non-physical aspects of her healing. After a short trial, she felt like she was not getting the results she was hoping for. She compared herself to other success stories and began to get down on herself. She eventually gave up and felt like a failure.

What happened here? She began a healthy juice cleanse to feel better rather than feeling like a failure. She forced results through the physical, completely ignored the non-physical. Then she ultimately gave up and felt the exact things she wanted to avoid. The law of attraction reflected back what she was holding on to, feeling like a failure. This is why it is important to work on the non-physical aspects as well. The emotional and energetic states will need to be released as you engage in a physical regiment. You will manifest the repressed energies that are being moved out physically. Pay attention to what shows up as you are working out. It is all being brought forward to feel better and raise vibration. If you are unconscious and unaware of it, you will ultimately end up feeling the exact things you set out to avoid. In this case, feeling like a failure.

## MANTRAS AND AFFIRMATIONS

I love mantras. I use them every day. They are power tools of sound and intention. Mantras are like bridges to the state of being you desire to experience. They can certainly help you get into the vibrational alignment that you desire. The sounds and the energy behind mantras can raise energy to a state of being. They help you keep your vibration at the level you want.

A major key to mantras is to feel the words that you are saying. What good are words if there are no intentions or energies behind them. All day long I can say, "I am loved," but it will not make a difference if I do not put energy behind and believe it. You must feel the words and what those words mean. You must embody the words and believe the sounds vibrating through you are true. You must experience the state of being through the mantra. Whatever mantra you decide is best for you, make sure you feel what you are trying to say.

Here are a few mantras or affirmations that can work with each chakra.

The Root:
- I accept my life as it is.
- I am grounded in my body.
- I am stable, safe, and secure.

The Sacral:
- I am creative.
- I am worthy.
- I allow myself to be open to others.

The Solar Plexus:
- I am strong and powerful.
- I allow peace.
- I accept myself.

The Heart:
- I forgive myself.
- I am loved.
- I allow love into my life.

The Throat:
- I am free to communicate.
- I freely express my truth.
- I communicate with ease and grace.

The Third Eye:
- I am living my manifestation.
- I see clearly.
- I am my inner vision.

The Crown:
- I am that I am.
- I am Source.
- I am connected to Source.
- I know by knowing.

My daily mantras are:
- I am love.
- I am divine light.
- I am will.
- I am abundant.
- I am supported by Source and all there is.

Again, I emphasize how important it is to feel what the intention is behind the mantras. For instance, when I say, "I am loved," I embody the energy and what it is like to be hugged and loved by the Universe as I say it. It becomes a vibrational experience rather than me just uttering out empty words. Once you embody the energy, take an action step with the energy. Create the next now moment with that energy. Seed your next now moment as the creator.

## LOVE YOUR WATER

Dr. Masaru Emoto was a Japanese businessman and author who conducted research on how human consciousness could affect the molecular structure of water. He tried to show us the impact human thoughts can have on water.

Water is like a liquid crystal. It holds the intention of the creator. For example, water will take on any shape or form based on external force. It will form a square if poured into a square box or it will become a circle if poured into a circle container. In addition, water can become forceful or gentle based on pressure applied to it. You can see that water can be shaped or programmed physically. It can also be programmed energetically, as Dr. Emoto showed us.

Think about holy water. When the element of water is blessed, it holds a higher vibration than water that is not blessed. Humanity can affect water. Water retains memory.

Your physical body is made up of mostly water. Water is in every part of your body right down to the cells. The liquid crystal that is water flows all throughout you. Every day you are thinking, talking, and acting out different intentions. Those patterns get reinforced into the water you hold. It is important to understand that you are programming the water in your body. Your body water holds the vibrational intention of your entire energy. It has become crystalized with how you are up until now. No wonder it is so hard to break a habit or a pattern!

### Water Exercise:

*Pour a glass of water. Place your left hand on your heart and your right hand over the glass of water. Imagine light entering into your crown down to your heart.*

**127**

*Imagine all this love in the form of golden light accumulating in your heart and then going down your right hand into the water. Send that love into the water. After you feel that the water is filled with love light, consume it.*

*What you are offering yourself is love in the form of water that you have projected onto it. It now holds the blessing of you and Source itself. The higher vibrational water will help you raise your frequency or interrupt the crystalized water stored in your body.*

*Be mindful that this exercise will expediate your healing. It is like you are fast-tracking your process. What you can find are old patterns that need to be released manifest immediately and powerfully. This is because the higher vibration forces the lower vibrations to be transmuted. It takes your awareness to not fall into the same pattern. This is why it is important to drink clean and clear water. So, love your water!*

## ALLOWANCE

I strongly emphasize the importance of inner work. The ability to look at your wounds or your traumas to help bring the energy to the surface. This begins the process of integrating the energy into a healing space. The inward journey is both discovery and integrations of energies.

Most of my experiences are about an inward journey about self-love. I talk about self-love a lot. I talk about self-worth a lot. They are one in the same, shades of the same color. It is truly important to look at these as the creator. It is deeply important that we move into those energies to understand how we developed those illusions about ourselves.

As a vibrational being, those beliefs within ourselves will pattern out in our lives. We spend a lot of time healing them, but what we forget is the allowance piece of that as well.

Sometimes we become hardened into the ways of our being to protect the vulnerability of our core issues. Once we uncover them, we understand how this has come about. Although we get an understanding of it, we don't know what to do with it.

It is like shining a light on the problem—you see it, you know it is there, but you do nothing about it. We keep shining light on it, keep showing it love, and yet we do not see much change. Why is that? Shinning a light on the problem is only half the solution. We must be willing to change it to see what we want. This would include changing our thoughts around the situation, changing the energy around the situation. You interact with it differently, your emotional place is different, and your physical body holds the energy differently as well. This means allowing that which needs to change to be changed.

In my particular experience, especially as an astrology sign sun rising Cancer, self-love is core healing for me. I long for love. The longing for deep connections. This is particular to my childhood and wanting to feel that from my parents. There is a deep level of pain that I have had to look at around this longing for love. I had to do the inner work, to look at this rejection or the sadness of not being accepted by my father and the feeling of abandonment by my mother. I developed an illusion about myself to keep me from feeling that.

This led me to deal with it in certain ways; create illusions about myself. I am a walking contradiction sometimes and here are some examples:

- As a parent, I want to be the provider. I want to be seen as someone who can do it all by themselves.
- I want to be independent.
- I choose to numb myself in relationships to lessen any pain of rejection or avoid feeling hurt.
- I am desperate to be loved and approved of but resent needing approval.
- I want to be free and am desperate to control my life.

You may want to be healing yourself, but you must also be open to allowing yourself to be in acceptance of that love as well. If you don't change the energy or the actions behind the love, then you will sit in the swirl of the same old patterns as well.

We must be willing to put ourselves out there as well. Allow ourselves to feel the openness of that love against all our internal resistance to that love. To open ourselves to change and to Source love that may cause further difficulties. For us to break out of an illusion, the illusion itself must break down as well. We must be willing to let go of the attachments of the previous you. We must be willing to allow new, unfamiliar things to occur, should we ever want to see life differently.

How can you feel love if you do not allow yourself to receive it? This means you have to be willing to open yourself up. In my experience, I had to learn how to:

- Let my guard down
- Trust someone
- Surrender
- Allow and receive help
- Allow myself to get close to people
- Allow myself to be vulnerable with people
- Stop numbing myself through alcohol and videos games
- Allow myself to be hugged and to hug others
- Connect with people

This all was a process. Each of these required me to revisit my beliefs and memories. In the end though, you have to allow good things to come. You have to allow yourself as the creator to create joy, peace, and love.

# KARMA

Karma in Sanskrit means "action" or "doing." In most cases, people understand it as the law of cause and effect. That which you do in this life will have an effect. The Buddhist expand the idea of karma to the intentional actions that will have an effect on this life and future life incarnations. My perspective on karma is it's an energy imbalance that requires balancing within this time and space.

The term karma has become humanized a bit. As most would see it, karma is the deserving repercussions of one's actions. Such that a person who does good deeds will receive good things in return, compared to those that do bad deeds will receive bad things in return. I have seen more times than not, people with good hearts receive bad things while people with bad hearts receive good things in return.

Karma is energy that is imbalanced and seeks to be rebalanced. Karma involves the law of attraction and the mirror. When you have energies that are repressed and rejected, they seek to be accepted and released. They seek to be rebalanced. They continue to be mirrored back to you until you as the creator shift your beliefs and release the energy. This can be expanded outwardly into your parallel lives as well as your ancestral lineage.

The important thing to understand is your life is being affected energetically. It is being affected by karma from parallel lives and karma passed down through your family lineage. Right now, your life is the sum of all your family lineage. Your physical vessel is the totality of all the DNA passed down from generation to generation. At some level you are integrating imbalanced energies in all those lifetimes. You are the sum of all your ancestral karma. It is quite a thing to consider and a big task to have to be the one to deal with it. You may not be conscious of the fact it is there, but it is playing out in your life somehow. Think about different themes that are part of your family lineage.

I typically see that a lot of emotional karma is passed down from the mother. It does not mean that the mother is always the one, it just happens to be the easiest to see. Mostly because the mother is the one with the children the most. The mother is also the physical vessel that represents the divine feminine energy which includes emotions. When the mother has certain emotional issues and emotional struggles, they will be unconsciously passed down to her child. Look at your mother and see what emotional patterns she was working with. The likelihood is that you are in some way living out the same emotionally repressed pattern in your life. That is why the old saying, "Cats have kittens and dogs have puppies," is true. You become an energetic replica of your parents because you are the unconscious projection of their traumas.

For instance, let's say your mother dealt with self-worth issues in her life. She never felt good enough. She would undoubtedly make her child feel unworthy as well. This is because her children would reflect her own self-worth issues that she projects onto them. It could look like holding the child to unattainable standards, repressing the child's emotions because they would bring unwanted attention, or incessantly making sure that the child looks proper. There are many things that could be unconsciously projected onto the child. The child would "inherit" the energy. The child would be a reflection

131

or catalyst of self-worth issues for the mother. Therefore, the child would never feel good enough. There would self-worth issues within herself and that would be reflected with her mother as well. It is a continuous transfer of the emotional trauma. Obviously, the father can be part of the process as well, passing his emotional karma down too, but in most cases the mother is the one because they care for the children more often. If you want a direct window into what patterns you hold, inquire about how your parents treated you and what your parents dealt with in their lives.

Most of us are unaware of our past lives, let alone the ancestry karma that we are dealing with. If you want to get an insight into your ancestral karma, take an honest look at your relationship with your parents. There will be a common theme playing out in your life that is present with the relationship you have with your parents. Or you can get a past life regression to gain access to memories that affect you now.

Karma lives within you and it does impact how you are. Knowing about these things can help you understand something about yourself, but it will not balance it. How do you balance it? Luckily, that is where you come in! You are the lucky one to do this! It is through you that the imbalanced karma can be neutralized. Through you can karma be balanced and removed. It is done by self-love and following the process outlined in this book. By making different choices than the patterns you typically fall into, you balance the karma.

You have the power in this moment to balance all of it. It takes the courage of self-love to become aware of repressed energies. It takes the courage of self-love to release these energies, so you do not have to hold on to them any longer. This will free you and heal you. This will free and heal your past lives. This will free and heal your ancestors.

## THE HIGHER SELF

The higher self is vital to knowing yourself. The way I interpret the higher self is Source energy that holds more of itself. It is a higher form of you that exists outside of space and time. It is you that has lived many different parallel lives. It is a fractal of Source but is removed from the limitation and attachments of the worldly/physical dimension.

Imagine a spoked wheel on a bike. In the center is where all the spokes combine. The higher self is the center where all the spokes come from. Each spoke represents the different lives or incarnations that the higher self has fractured out into. The spokes all shoot out and support the wheel or the circle. Right now, you are living one of those spokes that the higher self has sent consciousness into. You can see that there are many different spokes, and they all lead back to the higher self with spiritual experiences to fulfill Sources desires to know itself. This fractal-like experience continues back until it reaches Source itself. Your higher self is you, but it has more of Source within itself. It knows the truth of you as a soul that is an aspect of itself.

Your higher self has access to all the information and guidance that you are looking for. That is because your higher self is you. Your higher self has fractals of its consciousness living out different lives and experiences. Your energy is integrating many different lives simultaneously. There are other aspects of you living different experiences in different times and in different locations. You are affected by that energy, but you also are given the ability to tap into it for guidance. You must open your beliefs beyond our space and time construct. Think beyond your limited linear human life. It is all there and available and the higher self is part of it. Spend time getting touch with your higher self. There is much to be gained through yourself.

## Higher Self Exercise:

*Get into a meditative state (see Meditation section in Chapter 7). Imagine you are sitting in a chair surrounded by loving light beings. They are supporting you and offering you love. Imagine in the distance that a being begins to approach. The being is made of light. As the being slowly approaches, you start to sense the energy. Feel the light that is emitting from your higher self. Feel the ease, the lightness, the grace that flows from your higher self. Feel the love that surrounds you.*

*Straighten your spinal column and breathe deeply. Breathe into the energy that surrounds you and feel it integrate with you. Knowing all is well and all is perfect where you are. Feel the love.*

*You are your higher self. In this space, you may seek the guidance you need. What would you talk about with your higher self? What questions do you have? You may find your previous concerns and questions disappear. You may discover that there is no need to ask. This is because you, as your higher self, know the perfection of where you are. Your higher self understands the lesson and experience of what you are going through. Spend as much time as you wish. When you are done, offer love and honor for the time spent together.*

## SPIRIT GUIDES AND DREAMS

You are surrounded by a team of loving beings that support and guide you through life. This team does not exist in the same physical way as your so called "real-life" friends and family. Nevertheless, they are real indeed, and they are friends and family. They are here to assist you on your journey. They exist in a different vibration that is slightly outside of our physical senses, but they can still interact with you. It just takes us getting out of our own way to be able to communicate with them. Most of you know them as spirit guides. I would not be where I am today if not for my spirit guides. In some ways, your spirit guides are you, trying to help you. Your higher self is part of this team as well.

We are supported by a soup of energy that is Source. Source meets us where we are consciously in forms such us as spirit guides or other spirit forms to assist. There are spirit guides that stay with you through your life and there are some that come in for specific purposes. Your spirit guides are exactly that, they are guides. They are not dictators and do not force you into doing something. You have free will and they will honor your experience as a sovereign Source being. They will not infringe on your experience. That means you must ask for help or put your intention to connect with them. In addition, they will not give you the answers directly.

If you desire to get in touch with your spirit guides, I recommend meditation as a starting point to build a bridge to your guides. You need to create a space that is receptive to their communication and the meditative state is one way to do so. There needs to be a clear intention to create a space to meet and interact with your spirit guides.

## Spirit Guide Exercise:

*Set your intention that you desire to meet your spirit guides. Get into a meditation state. I would recommend that you start with a clearing protective golden light. Imagine that a bright golden light surrounds your body. Sit in that energy for a minute or two. Next, imagine that you are sitting at a table and that there are empty seats at the table. It can be any table with any kind of seats, whatever suits to your liking. Kindly ask that your guides step forward and show themselves to you. Invite them to sit with you. Let whatever image, feelings, or expression of energies come through. Imagine what they look like and what they sound like. Spend as long as you want with them. What kind of things would you ask?*

*I had a hard time with visualizing and trusting what I was experiencing. I found that my other senses were better for me. If this is the case for you, you could ask that your guides present themselves in a different way. Use your other sense to get to know them. For me, I would ask them to present themselves spatially to me. I would sense their presence in relation to my body. I would then use all my sense other than sight to help me understand their energy and get to know them.*

Many of you are not hardwired to interact with spirit or your spirit guides. There is no education about it in general. In fact, the opposite is imprinted on society. What you are told and shown through media such as television and movies is that spirit is an unknown dangerous thing. It will cause possessions and make you do terrible things. This leads to fear and fear creates all sorts of distorted perceptions of reality. It will block your connection and twist your interaction with spirit guides. Just because you do not know or have not experienced something before does not mean it is evil or negative. It just means you are experiencing it with no frame of reference. You must deal with your own stigmatism around spirit.

I remember a time when I was woken up in the middle of the night by spirit. I would feel this energy and sensation through my body. This was something new to me and I had no idea what was happening. I immediately took it as something negative was happening. I thought maybe it was demons or dark beings trying to possess me. My fear took me in that direction because of what I had seen portrayed in movies. It took some time to dissolve that fear construct and realize that my vibration was not at the same level as my spirit guides. What I was feeling was the adjustment of energy between me and them. Not demons.

The thing to remember—you are a vibrational match to the energy you carry. It is important to work on healing yourself to increase or raise your energetic vibration. As many things in our reality, spirit can also become a reflection of self. What you experience with any spiritual meeting can be, in many ways, a reflection of your own self. Take time to clear away aspects of yourself that may distort your interaction. Otherwise, you may have experiences that are like what I had above.

A much easier way for you to connect to your spirit guides is through dreams. Pay attention to your dreams. They can be important. I have received profound messages in dreams from my spirit guides as well as my higher self. Dreams can be more than just the brain running through your daily routines and concerns. It can be a place to have spirit communication.

It is far easier for spirit to communicate with you when you are in the dream state. It is often too difficult for you to receive messages when you are awake dealing with life. Your dream state can be the perfect place to deliver messages because you are disengaged from the physical world.

The brain wavelength while you are active is the beta wave. You have a lot of activity and are actively engaging in the physical world and your daily tasks. This is the most active brain wavelength because you are awake. Most are too preoccupied with life and the numerous activities that need to be done. It is difficult for your guides to reach you in this state.

The next brain wavelength is your alpha wavelength. Here, you are far more relaxed and detached from the activities of your daily life. You can let your mind rest and relax. The deep relaxing mindset when getting a massage or when you are meditating is associated with the alpha wavelength. In this wavelength you are far more open to receiving information and insight from your guides. You can sidestep your daily thinking and allow for other energies to meld with your mental and emotional body energies. This is why meditation works so well with getting messages or insight on things.

As you drift off to sleep, you are entering into the brain wavelength of theta.

This is the part of your sleep that is called rapid eye movement, or REM sleep. Here is where we enter into the so called "dreaming state." You are completely disengaged from the external physical world and dealing with the inner workings of your mind. This is where spirit has an easier time communicating with you because you are completely unplugged from the physical world and in a state that is open to receiving messages.

Spirit does not communicate in a linear sense like humans do. They do not communicate in the traditional sense of speaking to you directly in the English language or whatever your native language is. That is a human manifest of communication that is based on external vibration. Spirit is quantum and beyond space and time. Spirit will communicate in a way that can transcend time and space. In addition, there is free will. Guides cannot interfere with your free will. They may suggest something, but they will not interfere with your life. So, communication that leaves it up to you to decipher is a way to deliver messages without infringing on your free will. What can do that? This is through knowing, through symbolism, and through feelings. Pay attention to the things that are shown to you, things that you wake up knowing, or the way that you felt in the experience.

I feel there is a clear difference between a random dream versus a visitation or one that contains messages for you. It is through the vividness of the experience. I dream in color and when I am able to recall intricate details, especially the colors, I make sure to pay attention. What I have found is that spirit will project an experience for you to have. They will place you in a set of circumstances that make you feel a certain way. Think about a hologram that you were dropped into and experience. When the hologram is done running, you will be left with a knowing, symbolism to decipher, and feelings to digest during your waking state.

## Dream Journal Exercise:

*Get a dream journal. Write down what you remember from your dreams the minute you wake up. You remember much more right after a dream compared to later in the day. Doing this exercise will help you retain more from your dreams and not forget what was presented to you from spirit.*

## Dream Intention Exercise:

*Before you go to bed, put out the intention that you would like to remember what is important to you. Most of us go to bed without any intention and just fall asleep. If you want to remember your dreams and communicate with your guides, then consider putting out an intention to do so.*

*"I ask my higher self to recall my experiences tonight. I ask that I recall what is most important for me and my highest good."*

# FORGIVENESS

My biological mother died when I was around eighteen years old. I was not in contact with her for many years besides just receiving my annual birthday card. I was afraid to contact her. I could not face my own fears and pain. When she died, I had so much sadness and guilt within me. It was very hard for me to even think about my mother without crying and feeling the pain in my heart. It was easier to not face it. This built up a terrible guilt and shame. Guilt for not being a better son and shame for doing nothing to reach out to her. A multitude of things ate at me when she was alive, and we did not speak. It was hard lesson in love, if there is ever such a thing.

When she died, I was not able to let go of my guilt and shame. I held on to those feelings and was never able to forgive myself for my actions. The heaviness stayed with me until my mid-30s. Then I was forced to confront this guilt and shame.

I remember I had this relentless feeling of wanting to find an old photo of my biological mother. I asked my wife several times where it could be and she insisted it was in the attic. I searched through old boxes and containers for a couple of days. I finally found the photo and put it up in my office. Shortly after, my adopted mother gave me a letter that she had been holding on to for some time. It was a letter from my biological mother written before she died. It was heart-wrenching, and I felt all the underlying pain and sadness within me as I read each word. She wrote that she was going to go back to her family in Laos and that she would always love me. She never made it to Laos. I had to sit with myself and run through all the memories and my emotions.

Forgiveness is more for you than anyone else. It is for both parties involved, but you are the one that needs it the most. Whether it is about being forgiven or forgiving someone else, it is still about you. It is about allowing yourself to let go of energy that keeps you from moving on. Forgiveness is acceptance of what happened rather than rejection. It neutralizes the emotional charge left from the experience.

Most people find the forgiveness at the end of their process after truly accepting themselves. The forgiveness process can be quicker if you can step into the role of the creator and take accountability. When you become the creator, you immediately drop the victim mentality. You become empowered and see your experience from a different perspective. A more whole and loving perspective rather than a restricted, fragmented, fearful perspective. This place of consciousness understands why the co-created moment occurred. It was for both of you to understand yourselves as Source beings. At this juncture, you may offer forgiveness for yourself and for the other through love of self.

It is much easier to forgive or to receive forgiveness when someone is alive. It is much harder when someone is gone. Trying to receive forgiveness when there is no one to forgive or receive forgiveness from is like playing a multiplayer game by yourself. It is hard to realize that state when you are the one forgiving yourself. A word of advice from someone whose father and mother died before I got a chance to forgive or be forgiven—forgive while they are alive. Do not waste the opportunity while they are alive to let something go, heal, and move forward. Do not let things come between you and your own happiness because of grudges. The energy you are holding on to is far more destructive for you than it is for the counterparty. In most cases, the other person does not hold on to the same level of repressed energy that you do.

## GET USED TO COLORS

Did you know colors have a vibration? Of course they do! Just like the chakras within your energy system, each color has a vibration and a relationship to you. That is why it is important to find out what colors mean to you. Colors have a frequency. Each color of the rainbow has a specific frequency that it resides in. Red has a frequency of 400-484 Hz. Orange has a frequency of

484-508 Hz. The frequency increases for each color band of ROYGBIV until you get to violet, which ranges from 668-789 Hz. Each color has a different speed in relation to one another but are part of the whole which is white light.

These colors directly correlate with your chakra system. The lower chakra energy points relate more to the denser physical aspects of you. While the higher chakras relate more to the less dense etheric aspects of you. Is it of any surprise then to find that each chakra is perfectly aligned in frequency from low to high and attributed to the color that resonates to their specific frequency? There should be no surprise and it is not a coincidence.

Many of us resonate with a certain color at any given time, but in general we have an overall color hue that surrounds us. This is called the *aura*. The aura is the total makeup of your energy field and can provide information about yourself and others. Especially if you have clairvoyant abilities and can see the aura. It would be helpful to wear colors or surround yourself with colors that resonate with our aura. How do you know what the general color of your aura is? It is typically what feels best to you!

Most people wear a color or surround themselves with a color that is not in a vibrational alignment with their aura. It is not harmful to wear different colors, but it may dampen or create an energy dissonance. I compare this to someone who plays sports. Would it be better to play sports that you are talented at? Yes. That would be taking advantage of your gifts and using them to your advantage, rather than playing a sport that you are not talented at. That would require more work and it may not be as easy. When you use things to your benefit, things flow easier without much effort. You feel at home with it. Wearing a color that matches your aura is like going with the flow. It makes you feel better and lifts you up. That is why color therapy works. The resonance of the colors help you maintain a frequency that your aura holds rather than having a dissonance with it.

## Wear a Color Exercise:

*You can wear a certain color to highlight a certain chakra center. For instance, wearing the color blue can help you communicate more clearly. It helps activate your throat chakra and the energies can flow better. It helps you vocalize. Try wearing blue for a presentation to help you speak clearly and effectively or wear blue to help you communicate your truth in relationships. Having power struggles? Try wearing yellow to highlight your solar plexus chakra center and revitalize your power.*

## What Do Colors Feel Like Exercise?

*Grab a bunch of color samples. Make sure that each sample is complete with only one color. Spend time with each color in your hand. Hold one at a time and sense what you get from the color. This can help you understand what color you are resonating with and give insight into what mental and emotional blocks you might have. It may give you insight into what your aura color is.*

# GET OUTSIDE IN NATURE

You exist on Mother Earth. You are part of Mother Earth's energy and her physical body. Mother Earth is part of you. In some ways, you are Mother Earth, and she is you. We are one with each other. You cannot be separate if you are part of her energy field. How can a single cell be separate from the whole of the body? The cell functions and operates within its own reality, but it knows that it is part of the human form. The cell would cease to exist if you removed it from the body. The cell is dependent on the life force that the whole brings to it to survive and function.

Mother Earth provides us everything. It is only through unconditional love and life force that we are afforded all we need to survive and thrive on her. We are dependent on all aspects of her. We need her air, we need her water, we need her physical body, and we need her energy. Everything that we see around our reality is in some way or form a co-creation with Mother Earth.

Energy is provided freely because you are her, much like you are Source. Her love is neutral. It is love with no conditions. In the physical sense, you are surrounded by her divine love. The trees, the water, the air, the mountains, the oceans, etc. Nature is a direct link to Source love. Nature is a healing love energy. It is also a grounding energy because it helps you feel safe within the body. When you feel loved, you feel safe. When you feel safe, you can be present in your body and in the moment.

Get out in nature. Make this a daily practice because you will feel safer in your body. You will be more grounded and present with yourself. A lot of things can shift by just going for a walk in nature.

### Nature Exercise:

*Go for a walk outside, preferably in nature or in natural areas. Focus on your senses as you move through nature. Notice what you see, what you smell, what you feel, and what you hear. Be present with your senses.*

*Notice the difference between how you felt before your walk and after your walk.*

## SYNCHRONICITIES

I do not believe in coincidences. I believe in a loving and supportive Universe. I believe that you are loved because you are Source. Since you are Source, you are supported with the power to create. As you create your reality, you will ultimately see signs of alignment with what you are building. You will see synchronicities of the Universe aligning with your vibration. A synchronicity is having a signal or a validation from the Universe. Think about what happens when people come together to synchronize their watches. We come together so that our timing is aligned and matched up. This is like getting together with the Universe and synchronizing your watch, except it does not involve time. It involves energy and vibration.

Throughout your life, you may have found that certain things, events, and experiences lined up a certain way. They lined up, against all odds, in a way that you became aware of. You recognized within your awareness that something was weirdly happening and made note of the coincidence.

To me there is meaning to everything, even down to the smallest pebble. There is purpose in our lives and the Universe provides signs for it. What you witness and experience is filtered through your energy. At some level there is purpose. There is meaning behind experiences that we have and that depends on what meaning you decide to give them.

Synchronicities can come in any form. They can be anything that you put meaning into. Synchronicity in numbers, animals, objects, people, colors, etc. The thing to remember is that synchronicities are always occurring. They are always occurring because you are always creating.

What many misunderstand about synchronicities is they believe that they only go one way. There is a sense of judgement toward your creations. Judgement of your creations as good or bad, positive or negative, light or dark. When you experience something that is not in alignment with what you want it is labeled as bad or negative. You say, "This does not make me feel good. I must not have created it." Or you look at your experience and reject it all together while labeling it as a negative sign. Yet, when you experience something that is in alignment with your desires, you say, "This makes me feel good. Look at what I created!" You accept what you are creating and take the sign as a good thing. We have become bias to synchronicities, when in fact everything is a synchronicity helping you understand yourself.

We must remember the mirror. You are learning about yourself through your experiences. It is your own energy and judgments that give meaning to the synchronicity. What if you considered the concept that synchronicities are always happening and that they are always good? It is only confirming what your beliefs are and it takes you as the creator to see that. That perspective would offer more insight into who you are without much resistance.

I remember an experience where I was dealing with a failing septic system. It was just another experience where I was shelling out money. I took the experience as a negative event. I was angry and felt like a victim because it was going to cost me several thousands of dollars for a hole in the ground.

One could look at my septic system fiasco and say it was a negative synchronicity. That experience was bad and ultimately to be rejected. This is how most people tend to think regarding these so-called negative experiences. What if they were not negative synchronicities? Suppose we looked through a different perspective of a positive synchronicity highlighting my victimhood belief. How does that change your perspective of the event? If we remove the judgement of good or bad from synchronicities, then we can find the truth of what they are. Synchronicities are energetic alignments of your beliefs.

# CHAPTER 8:
# START CREATING CONSCIOUSLY

My spirit guide and I stood there talking to each other for some time. We were standing among a beautiful landscape, one that felt serene and natural. It was open, like being at a state park with a few homes and buildings around. At one point in our discussion, I asked my spirit guide in a sarcastic tone, "So what am I supposed do? Just sit here and vibrate?!" My spirit guide calmly turned her attention to me with an assertive look. "Look around you," she said. I turned my attention to the landscape all around us. As I looked and noticed what was before me, my guide reassured me with the emphatic truth, "This is all a vibration."

It became clear to me in that moment that our world is just energy vibrations at different speeds giving the illusion of separation. It also became clear to me that we affect our reality by our vibrational output. You affect your reality through how you hold yourself. The vibration or the energetic intention you hold creates an outward shift and bends your reality. Your vibration is magnetizing the physical world into your experience. This is the truth of our reality shared to me by my guides. Your consciousness is driving it.

At all times you are creating your vibrational experience. Whether you like it or not or whether you are aware of it or not, you are actively participating in creating your experiences. Even with experiences with other people, you are co-creating that experience which is happening in your reality. That is how powerful you are. You are not a victim to life. Life happens because of you.

We are like builders. We are natural creators and builders of life. When you desire something to build, we call forth the things we need from the Universe. The Universe is like a giant warehouse of materials waiting for us to place the ticket order. Things would flow better and be more efficient if we knew what we were writing down on the ticket order to the Universe. Imagine being a builder and having no sense of what supplies you are ordering from the warehouse. You would get a delivery of random materials and equipment at your construction site. It would be utter chaos and there would be no way to build what you want.

So why go through all these awareness exercises? Why try to work on healing your traumas and processing your emotions? Why bring your deepest darkest secrets into the light? Is all this work for naught? No. It is so you can build and create consciously with the Universe rather than unconsciously. The exercises are to help you retake charge of your life. That you no longer recreate patterns from unconscious states of repressed emotional energy. It is to help you be the builder you want to be and become conscious of the ticket order you are writing to the Universe. You are truly creating your reality and are one hundred percent accountable for what you do in the now moment.

This is all a process to become the creator that you are. A rediscovery of the truth and the power the lies within. It is a process of awareness of your thoughts, beliefs, and actions. An awareness that empowers you to create the life you deserve. A life that is in alignment with more joy, peace, and love in your life. Now that you have the awareness of the blueprint, you can change your life.

Once you become aware of your unconscious beliefs, you must clean house. You must make space and allow room for the new you. To do so requires you to clear out old energy. You must take the old you and clear things out. You must adjust your vibration so that you do not recreate the same patterns in your life that you vehemently reject.

Now that you are clearing or working on clearing dense unconscious energies, you can put energy where you want it to go. You can focus intentionally without the weight of your traumas keeping you from feeling the heights of joy and love. You are no longer held back by the unconscious aspects contributing to your overall vibration. You can align with your desires without fear of the past.

Let us talk about your fear and love. As you are keenly aware by now, the first mode of operandi is to understand that you are the creator. The second is to understand your beliefs. A lot of those beliefs are old traumatic beliefs that needed to be uncovered. Energies that needed to be brought to the surface and integrated.

Your beliefs come in two forms: fear and love.

Each of these energies are extremely powerful, but one is limiting. Can you guess which one? Fear. Fear energy is a powerful energy. Perhaps just as powerful as love, but it is limiting. Fear is contracting, constricting, and restrictive. Think about the energy of fear and how it affects you. When was the last time you were angry? Did you think about other people's feelings in that angry state? Do you recall wanting to help others? Do you recall the ability to see anything but red? That is fear energy. It contracts and limits your energy. It pinches you off from Source. It limits your perspective and reduces the amount of light you can hold or take in. In doing so, you miss out on all the other things outside the box. This is why you cannot persuade people into understanding certain things, because their limited beliefs in fear keep them from integrating or seeing outside their understanding. Draw a circle around yourself and that is your symbolic understanding of fear. It can only see within the circle. It cannot move outside the circle. It is finite.

Now think about love energy. Love energy is expansive. Love extends beyond self. It opens and broadens your perspective and energy. It is cooperative and infinite. Think about the energy of love and how it makes you feel. When was the last time you were happy? Love allows you to move beyond the self. You can think about others or consider other people. You are compassionate and understanding. Your vision opens up as compared to being tunnel-visioned or myopic with fear. You can find solutions that were not there before because you can think outside of the box.

Fear is just an acronym for False Evidence Appears Real (F.E.A.R.). If you were to examine the fear behind your motivation you would find most fears are illusions. The fear we hold contains far worse outcomes than what we actually experience in reality. In addition, that fear holds no water. What you are experiencing is an illusion that is causing you to think in a limited way. You are taking the infinite Universe and constricting it down to a narrow bandwidth.

In 2005, the National Science Foundation published an article regarding research about the number of thoughts we have per day. The average person has about 12,000 to 60,000 thoughts per day. What they found was eighty percent of peoples' thoughts were negative and ninety-five percent of those thoughts were exactly the same repetitive thoughts as the day before. When you are unconscious about yourself, you are basically a negative person with eighty percent of your thoughts focused on fear, the same fear you had the day before and the day before that.

Think about the body of water metaphor and your thoughts being rocks. Your body of water is constantly rippling from throwing negative rocks. It is rippling from negative thoughts that are repetitive of the same fearful concerns. Sixty thousand thoughts per day is an energetic force to be reckoned with. Sixty thousand rocks splashing your body of water can create a tsunami.

When you are in fear, you start to worry and have anxiety about the future. You fear what the future outcomes can be. As a creator, you are putting all your intention and energy into manifesting limited realities or timelines that are based in fear. Not only are they based in fear, but your intention and energy are restricting your realities to the worst-case scenarios. Think about that. When you are in fear you are literally trying to manifest your worst-case scenario. You think about the worst things, you start changing your behavior around those thoughts, and you take actions like those things are going to happen. Do you want to manifest the worst things for yourself? Probably not, but that is what you are doing. There are far better realities or timelines you can manifest or experience. More positive and love-based realities.

Think about how different your life would be if you were conscious of your thoughts. The different choices you would make out of love rather than those choices motivated by false evidence appearing real. The negative thoughts that keep you from doing things, keep you from your desires, that keep you small and limited would shift. Imagine what 60,000 thoughts or rocks of love energy could do to your life. You would see your life change right before your eyes. You would have imaginable shifts to your life all because you align yourself with positive love energy. You would focus on your opportunities and strength and live life with more joy and fulfillment.

There can be great change when one sits in meditation and consciously aligns their entire energy field toward an intention. I have seen this work out in many different scenarios. I remember my wife was dealing with a bunch of self-worth issues. She was experiencing the same energy one right after another. It was especially profound for her when she was getting her hair colored one day. After spending hours at the salon, her hair color was not how she wanted it. It was extremely frustrating as she had clearly explained what she wanted but it came out wrong anyways. In addition, this was not her first time at this place. She felt like a failure and was completely down about her physical appearance. She made another appointment hoping to fix it. Before her appointment she was having all sorts of emotional expressions about her self-worth. She reached out to me for help. She became aware that there was something trying to be seen with the patterned experiences. Unfortunately, she did not have time to digest it all in our conversation. With the time she had, I instructed her to sit and meditate on what it would feel like to feel good. To feel a memory where she felt the best. To feel what she wanted and bring the energy into her now moment. She did as I instructed and went to her appointment. Sure enough, her hair color came out right and it was free of charge. She felt good. Now that might be a coincidence to you, but I have seen that work for so many people. We have the power to move through our experiences with fear or love. That choice is yours.

## Love or Fear Exercise:

*Take a moment and reflect about what you are thinking and doing right now? Is what you are doing motivated by fear? Is it a limited belief? Does it harbor lower vibrational emotions such as anger? Fear? Anxiousness? Stress? How does your body feel? Does it feel tense? Stiff? Is there dis-ease or imbalance in your energy? Is the fear real?*

*Or are your thoughts or beliefs motivated by love? Do you feel more joy? Happiness? Empowerment? Is your body at ease? Balanced? Does it feel light?*

## VISUALIZE

In tangent with meditation, visualization is an extremely powerful process. It has been shared through many different fields that mediation and visualization can improve performance or create desired outcomes. I know that for many sports athletes, visualization is common practice. They visualize their desired outcomes and focus on that energy during their games. Visualization can be a power tool, but it is not the full picture.

Here is something to understand before you try manifesting. There is a saying in the spiritual community, specifically an old Hebrew proverb, "There is nothing new under the sun." The proverb means that what has been done has been done and will be done again. There is nothing new to be discovered. This saying is referring to the human hyperbole that things tend to repeat itself. I want to take that a step further beyond the idea of the monotony of our human existence. Expand your consciousness a bit further. Expand yourself beyond your human container.

You understand that you are from Source or from all that there is. What makes you and me is the energy that surrounds us that is Source. Within Source, you cannot have something that is not Source. It is all within Source. All that there is and will ever be is within Source. Every thought that has been thought of and all that has ever been created or will be created already exists within Source. It exists right now as part of Source. Therefore, as a fragment of Source, you can access all that there is. This includes vibrational experiences that you desire. These desires that you wish to experience already exist within the present moment because all the experiences which can be thought of already exist. It is a matter of vibration and frequency.

As a vibrational being, you magnetize experiences based on what your frequency is matching to. You draw into your reality vibrational timelines or experiences that align with how you think, feel, act, and believe in. You are not creating, per se, a new experience for yourself. Instead, what you trying to do is align yourself to vibrationally match an experience that is already there. Like I said, there is nothing new under the sun. There already exists an experience or timeline where you are experiencing the exact thing you are desiring.

For example, imagine a piano. Within the piano are all these strings that play different notes. Each string is set to a certain note or frequency. These represent timelines that your experience could have. Imagine now that there are infinite strings. Within each moment, you are holding on to different frequencies. These frequencies are the sum of what you are holding on to. Let us say you are resonating on single note on the piano, C in the 4th octave. So as the creator you are constantly hitting the C4 key. You will maintain that note or in our example, the timeline, until you decide to change it.

The next now moment, you shift your resonance because you start thinking negatively about your life and begin to act differently than before. You now start hitting a lower piano key, B4. Different note. Different timeline. Or, instead of thinking negatively, you start thinking more positively about your life. You now move higher on the scale and hit the D4 piano key. Different note. Different timeline. Now think about how many different thoughts and emotions you have about your day. This gives you a sense of how much you are jumping around in vibrations. It would be like you are playing piano to one of Beethoven's piano concertos.

In a sense that is what is happening at every now moment. Depending on what you are feeling, thinking, acting, and believing in you are constantly moving around on different piano strings or timelines. Now think about this—there are octaves to these piano scales. Ones far greater and ones far lower, from a linear standpoint. These all could represent vastly different lives that you cannot fathom or imagine. All these experiences that your life could have been or would have been. They are all happening now, it is just you are energetically and vibrationally focused on this very place, at this very moment in time and space, because it serves you best.

Most of us go about our day thinking unconsciously about our own vibration, let alone matching timelines. We have no idea that we are choosing our timelines at every single moment. It is in the moment that we must be conscious about ourselves because in every now moment is all that there is. All that there is, is now. No past or future. It feels like linear time because we are just stringing each now moment together to give us the illusion of time. Yet, throughout our day we are constantly jumping around choosing different now moments that align with different timelines and realities. The amazing thing is that most do that without any idea they are doing it or being conscious of it. Think about how much you could shift your reality if you were conscious in each moment.

The law of attraction comes into play because the Universe is drawing into your reality the timelines that hold what you are desiring. In each now moment, the potentials can be drawn in like a giant ball of yarn with infinite strings. You end up on the most likely string based on your free will, thoughts, emotions, and overall energetic frequency. Remember that there are infinite timelines that spring forth from the now moment. What you experience are those timelines of the greatest probability based on current vibrations.

How do you tap into the other strings or timelines? Visualization. This helps unlock the portal to the timeline that you are looking to experience. You are visualizing experiences that you would like to have. The fact that you can imagine it means that it is within the realm of consciousness and can be brought forward. Visualizing helps shift your resonance to match the frequency.

Visualizing alone will not manifest the timeline you are looking for. It is only part of the equation. That is why I say you need to work on yourself to become aware. You need to become aware of how you think, how you feel, what you believe in, what your energies are, and how you are acting in the moment. If these are not in alignment with what you are trying to manifest, then it will be difficult to manifest the experience that you desire. Even more difficult is maintaining the vibration on a consistent basis. Throughout your day, you will undoubtedly get bumped off course, jumping into another timeline that is not aligned with your desires.

That is why manifesting materialism via the law of attraction can be such a trap. A trap because you spin your energy and get unbelievably upset or frustrated when things are not the exact thing you are looking for. Take winning the lottery for example. We all can use our imagination. How many times have you tried to visualize winning the lottery? Why does it not work out for most of us? There could be several reasons, but the primary is that you are not a vibrational match to it. You do not vibrationally match the experience of winning the lottery, nor can you hold the vibration long enough to align with that timeline. Trying to do so will only deflate you and perhaps delude you from seeing your true power. And in fact, as you should now understand, the experience of not manifesting the lottery winning was exactly what was needed. Even if one does win, the likelihood is they go bankrupt five years later. This is because it is too much at one time and they cannot handle what money does to them.

My hope is for you to focus your energy on more constructive areas, such as your state of being. Working on yourself to remove the limited distortions or traumas in your life to focus on the good rather than the bad. To work on yourself to be happy no matter what the law of attraction brings to you. As long as the experience makes you feel joy, peace, love, happiness, and empowerment, then it really does not matter what or how it comes to you.

Let us revisit fear in relationship to timelines. When you are in fear about the future, you worry. You worry about how things can go wrong and get anxiety about what it may hold. You fear future outcomes. This takes you out of the now moment and out of your body. As a creator, you are putting your intention into a future manifestation or timelines that are based in the worst-case scenarios for you. Think about that. You are literally trying to manifest your worst-case scenario. Do you want to manifest the worst thing for yourself? Probably not. There are far better constructs or timelines you would rather experience, but that is what fear does. Fear is not just affecting your mental body. It affects everything.

Your mental body is now thinking about the worst-case scenarios. Your emotionally body is in imbalance with anxiety and feeling scared about the worst-case scenario. This all tells the physical body to follow suit. You get shallow breathing, your adrenaline starts pumping, your muscles tense up and your heart rate goes up. Your entire energetic system is now in full alignment with itself. It all becomes a powerful alignment for manifesting. Except you are manifesting your fearful intentions. That is why the things we fear the most typically self-manifest.

I remember a financial planning client of mine whose worst fear was that they would have to spend all their money on health care. It was a constant concern and fear that they had. Well, guess what manifested?! The client ended up with long term care issues and is now spending their entire life savings on their health care costs. These things are not coincidence. It is you, as the powerful creator, manifesting your intentions.

I remember a time that I had very little money and I was just starting out in a new job. I was on my way to visit a prospect in my car. I was short on money and had to forego my car inspection until I got the money. It made me a fearful mess. Every time I got into my car I was fearful that I would get pulled over. I was fearful that I did not have the funds to pay the ticket and get my car inspected. I was so fearful that I constantly checked my speed and was worried that there was a police car behind every bend. What happened? Sure enough, my fears came true. I was pulled over by a brand new police officer that managed to catch my outdated inspection sticker while driving at speeds of 55 MPH.

Do not discount your creator power and the ability to affect your future timelines. You are the creator creating your timeline in every moment. Honor it and empower yourself.

## ABUNDANCE

The vast majority of people focus on the idea of manifesting material abundance into their lives. This is because they believe in some fear belief that is limiting their ability to have abundance or feel abundance.

I have spent nearly fifteen plus years working in the financial industry helping people manage their financial affairs. I have worked with incredible people with all different ranges in material wealth. The majority of my clients had more wealth than the average middle class person. What I found is that the more money you have does not equate to more happiness. It does not make you happier. It certainly helps you get things to make life easier or more convenient, but it does not equate to a more peaceful and happier life.

For instance, I recall a client who had millions to in net worth. They had several homes and millions in financial accounts. Their biggest fear was that they would end up panhandling for food on the side of the road. This fear or limited belief restricted them from feeling abundance even though they had millions to their name. They worried so much and were constantly trying to protect their money. They were retired and should have been enjoying a life of financial freedom and happiness. Unfortunately, it was completely different. There was constant worry and a fulfilling life eluded them. In the end they had massive health issues and were spending their wealth on that.

The lack mentality limits people from feeling more financial abundance. One of my major limited belief was around lack and feeling like a survivor. Growing up with little or no money, lack was a constant theme. We were always just trying to survive on some level. My biological immigrant parents' only possessions were what they brought on their back. My adopted parents were struggling financially as well. My father was going through a major bankruptcy with his business and my mother was an elementary educator, all while trying to raise five children. You can imagine some of the struggles. This lack mentality was imbedded within my beliefs.

There was I time I had a huge argument with my wife, before we were married. I was renting an apartment in an urban area. I had just started working for a new financial company and was starting to make more money than I ever had before. At that time, my windows in my bedroom did not have any blinds. My wife kindly suggested that blinds were needed so that people could not see into my room.

I was immediately triggered. I said, "We don't need them! I grew up without them and therefore they're not necessary." At which she immediately began to question why she was dating me. After some logical reasoning and threating to leave me, I agreed. So, we went out to find blinds at the local hardware store and I said we only need "cheap-o depot" ones, pointing to the cheapest ones available.

I took on a lack limited belief that kept me feeling like I needed to survive. I only needed the essentials. If it was not essential, then it was not needed. If I had a bed, some food, and clothes on my back then I should not complain. Anything more is excess and materialistic. How can I feel abundance when I am about lack mentality? How could I thrive when I focused on surviving?

You need to look at the concept of abundance and the definition you hold around abundance. What does abundance mean for you and how it involves money? The truth is you are not looking for abundance. For an abundance of nonsense items is just clutter and does not serve you. What you are looking for is the state of being that abundance allows. You are looking for the underlying feeling that abundance brings.

This is indeed another level to your self-awareness. What does abundance mean for you and how does money play into that? From what I have learned and seen in my experience is that money, or the concept of money, is a great enhancer of your beliefs. What money does to people is enhance their emotions, enhance their beliefs, and enhance their law of attraction experiences.

For instance, I dealt with a lot of self-worth issues. What money did in my reality was enhance the feeling I was not worthy. I remember trying to buy workout pants and having an issue around it. I wanted to buy myself new ones because my other ones were worn out. I found a workout pant that I liked and wanted to buy. I liked the way they looked and I liked the way they felt. But when I went to look at the price tag, I was taken back by the sticker price. Even though I was making good money, I refrain from buying it saying "I should not spend money on this!" In turn, I bought a lower quality workout pant for less money. I ended up being completely unhappy with them. The whole experience was an enhancer of my unworthiness via the construct of money. I did not feel worthy enough to buy the workout pant even though I liked them and needed new ones. I thought I did not deserve to spend that kind of money on myself, especially for workout pants. I allowed money to enhance my feelings of unworthiness over a few dollars.

Take another example, my belief in lack. Money enhanced this limited belief. I recall I was trying to cut cable out of my budget. I was thinking about how much my cable bill was and how expensive it was. I went through the whole process of trying to save money. I researched what I had to do and what I needed to do. By the end of the whole process, I realized that it was going to save me $40-$60 a month. Now, by this time I was making six figures. I was trying to save $40-$60 per month because I felt like my cable bill was so expensive. I realized I was focusing on lack. Lack mentality kept me from appreciating that I could afford the cable and I was already abundant. I was focused on trying to save a buck rather than being grateful that I could afford my cable.

Money is a great enhancer. If you want a nice window into what your beliefs are, look at your relationship with money.

## MONEY IDENTITY

Money is a great enhancer. You will just magnify or enhance your unconscious beliefs. You must understand the belief keeping you from feeling abundance. It is an underlying belief that you are projecting out. You need to get through that before you can bring abundance to you. In addition to abundance, you must look at the concept of money itself. Many of you have definitions around money that limit your abundance.

What exactly is money anyways? Do you understand what money is? In the United States we have the dollar bill. What exactly is the dollar bill? It is a piece of paper. It is a piece of paper that has writing on it. In fact, it says on the dollar that it is a "note" of the United State Treasury. A note is debt. The dollar is a piece of paper that represents debt. You do not hold anything of value. You hold debt. Is debt worth anything? No. That is why it is called a bill. You bill someone for the debt that you have incurred. A lot of people are giving their power away to something that is considered debt and is worthless. They are giving their power away for a piece of a paper. Perhaps the reason you do not have abundance is because you are desiring paper that represents debt.

We, as creators, have many ways to receive abundance from Source or the Universe. It can come in any form if we are open to it. The physical means of receiving abundance through currencies, like the dollar, is a very limiting way of allowing Source abundance into your life. You have limited the Universe to just one narrow pathway. You are essentially taking the infinite Universe down to a pin head. That is a lot of restricting for trying to feel abundant.

In doing so, you have given your happiness and peace to a piece of paper that is literally worthless. This closes you off from experiencing abundance or receiving abundance from the Universe in any other form. There are many different ways to feel abundant. It does not have to be confined to the definition of the dollar. You are missing out on feeling abundant because of this narrow definition. If you open up your concept around abundance you might find that abundance was right in front of you.

In addition, we must look at your beliefs around money as well. My perspective about money was distorted by my negative beliefs around it. I developed an idea that money is bad or evil. I thought that it was a bad or evil thing to want money and materialistic things. How many of you have the idea money is bad or evil? There is an old adage that states the root of all evil is money. How many times have you heard that? I heard it enough to think it was true. Nowadays, I would agree on some level, but I would say that is not all true. Money is a human construct needed to help us transact. Just like anything else that you manifest into your life, it reflects self. Money is not an evil thing. It is a tool and like all tools, it can be used for our highest good or not for our highest good. People with unconscious beliefs that are based in negative concepts will have money issues. When you no longer attach to those deeply charged beliefs around money, things will shift.

Money can be seen as an exchange of energy. Energy likes to flow. It does not like to sit still or be held back. The more energy that flows the more magnetic it becomes. You must look at money differently should you desire more abundance. The vast majority hold onto it like it is everything. Almost like if you lose it, it will never come back. Think about how that belief around money is playing out. It is lack mentality. It is fear. How can you have abundance if you fear losing it? The energy does not match. Something must change if you want to allow more abundance into your life, otherwise you cannot hold onto it.

## Charity Exercise:

*Let us imagine you are driving a car and come to a stoplight. There is a person panhandling in need of cash. In your wallet, you have several bills that sum up to $100. You have $1s, $5s, $10s and $20s.*

*Without thought as to what the person will do with the money, what amount would you give? Did you gift less than what you have? Why? Is it because of fear? Was it lack mentality that limits you? If you want to be abundant, then you must believe you are abundant. One who is abundant trusts and knows that they have more than enough. They know they will receive abundantly from the Universe. They would openly and willingly give the total sum of $100 because they know* *they are abundant. Next time you actually see someone in need of cash, see what thoughts and emotions come up.*

Try to follow my awareness exercises but focus primarily on memories about money. This could help you discover what your beliefs are about abundance and money.

Once you have discovered the underlying issues with money, follow the process within Chapter 6. It is important to really feel what abundance is for you in Step 3 of the process. What would it feel like to have the things you want? How would it feel in the body? Really get into the visualization of what you want to manifest.

## FORM STOPS YOU

One of the biggest blocks to you receiving what you want is form. It is human nature to desire things and to place your belief in how they are supposed to come to you. You want them to show up in a certain way. You want to it now and it cannot be anything but what you imagine it to be.

There are a few things that we must remember:

1. The Universe or Source energy is infinite and abundant.
2. The Universe or Source energy is efficient and effective.
3. The Universe matches vibration and frequency.

The Universe is infinite. It is not limited. It can bring you whatever you want. It is your belief system that is limiting the Universe. The Universe is infinitely open to you.

The Universe is efficient and effective. It will bring experiences to you in the most efficient and effective manner. Also remember this, it takes the same amount of energy to manifest a penny and to manifest a million dollars. It is your belief that makes it seem different.

As you already know, it is imperative to understand that what you are looking to manifest into your life is a gateway to a vibrational state of being. It is not necessarily the thing you are trying to manifest but rather the state of being you are trying to experience. For instance, let us say you want to manifest a million dollars. You want abundance and you want it in the form of a million dollars. The million dollars is the gateway to the state of being you are trying to experience. So, as I have said above, what does the million dollars represent to you? Why do you want the million dollars? What feeling will you have when you have a million dollars?

This is critical to the process. Let's say that the million dollars represents freedom. If you get a million dollars, you do not have to work anymore or you can freely travel. This is the underlying emotion or vibration that you are trying to achieve. This is what you are looking for.

When you say you want freedom and tie it to a form, such as a million dollars, you are restricting or limiting the first two points about the Universe. One, you have taken the infinite and restricted it to a finite pathway. Two, you have then reduced the effectiveness and efficiency of the Universe to deliver the experience to you.

The last point is the Universe does not care about the million dollars. The Universe cares about matching the vibrational output you are desiring. The Universe can and will bring the matching vibrational expression in infinite ways to you. In more ways than you are conscious about, but you have to be open to it.

Imagine that you are asking for a present from the Universe. You want it in a square white box wrapped in a red ribbon. This box represents freedom to you. Now the Universe, in its unconditional love, says, "Fine." It starts bringing you freedom but this time it comes a in blue square box with a red ribbon. Since it is not what you want, you ignore it. Then comes a rectangle white box with a red ribbon. It is close but not what you are looking for. You see what is happening here? The Universe knows you more than you do and knows what that vibrational experience looks like. The present you are looking for can come in a different shape, different color, and with different color ribbons. In fact, it may not even be in a box, it could come in a bag, or gifted wrapped in wrapping paper. The point is, there are infinite ways, but you are attached to form. The attachment to form restricts your ability to receive. You need to get out of your own way. You need to stop focusing on form and start allowing the Universe to bring you experiences that match your vibrational desires no matter the form.

## Daily Exercise:

1. Identify what abundance feels like for you.
2. Now that you know what you are looking or feeling for, it is time to be mindful of it. The first thing to do is become aware when the feeling is showing up in your reality. You have to acknowledge that you and Source energy, or you and other co-creators, or you alone, created an experience that brought the feeling you are looking to experience. It requires you to be aware and conscious of what is happening in your reality. How can you acknowledge something good or that is a vibrational match to your desires if you remain unconscious throughout your day?
3. Next you need to give gratitude when you have it show up. You've got to be thankful that it is occurring or has occurred. This reinforces that idea and the vibration you are experiencing. It allows you to maintain the frequency.
4. Lastly, you must allow for the Universe to keep bringing the experience to you in whatever form it can.

There was a time I wanted to feel financial freedom in my life. The ability to do what I wanted and not have to care about how much I was spending. I was thinking about millions, a private plane, and traveling all over the world. I was putting the form of financial freedom on having millions of dollars, like winning the ultimate jackpot in the lottery. I would imagine the details of it and what the money could buy. I would daydream about these things. Financial freedom had to come in large lump sums of money for me to feel that state of being. All I would think of was that narrow pathway of winning the lottery. There was no other option for me in my mind.

It took me some time to examine my perspective around financial freedom. I noticed I had closed myself off from feeling this state of being due to form. I closed myself off from feeling any sort of financial freedom even though I was already abundant. When I was able to focus on the feeling and let go of form is when things shifted for me. I was able to find gratitude and appreciation for experiences that made me feel financially free. I felt gratitude when I went to the grocery store. I was grateful to buy our weekly groceries without much thought to what I was spending. I was deeply appreciative of the experience of buying lunch or being able to go for a walk outside. I felt financially free in that moment. Little by little I became more aware of the abundance I had in my life. I started to allow the Universe to bring me more experiences to continue that feeling. When you can let go of form and allow is when you can open your perspective to the state of being you desire in the moment. It is all there for you now. You just need to let go of form.

In the previous chapter I talked about allowing. Trust that the Universe will bring the experience. Trust that it will come. You just need to be open to it. Focus on the state of being that you want rather than the form.

## OUT WITH THE OLD, IN WITH THE NEW

Your entire life you have held on to a certain vibration that has brought you to where you are now. The sum of all your energy is why you are right where you are. As we have said, your best decision making is the reason you are where you are. If you are looking to change something about your life, you must change something about you.

You must make room for something new. This means you must remove or change something about yourself to be in alignment with what you want. Otherwise, you will never be in alignment with what you want because you never changed your frequency. You will not be a match for that vibrational experience.

Imagine someone who is overweight and trying to become healthier. They want to lose weight and feel better about themselves. They spend much of their time on the couch eating junk food which makes them feel crappy about themselves.

What does the person need to do to experience what they want? They need to work out, they need to change their diet, and they need to work on themselves to feel better. This person basically needs to change their entire vibration to become the vibrational match to what they want. This person cannot just sit there visualizing and feel what they want and expect their life to change. What change can occur by thinking about being in better shape while sitting on the couch eating junk food? Nothing has changed. They will remain as is until something changes.

You must change. You must become a match to what you want. You must remove an old aspect of yourself that contributed to the overall vibration to become a different one. What are you doing to put yourself in alignment with the vibrational experience you want? How are you changing yourself to be a match?

## SPIRITUAL GROWTH AND MATERIALISM

The essence of Source running through you is seeking to know itself. It seeks spiritual growth in experiences. In the world of form, there is only so much the soul can learn from materialistic possession. Possessions and accumulations of material things only bridge so far in your spiritual fulfillment. That is why you find so many people who are unbelievably wealthy but are unbelievably unhappy. Remember that money enhances one's beliefs.

You hear stories about people who win the lottery and go bankrupt five years later. The idea of winning the lottery seems blissful but, in most cases, it just enhances the issues they hold. They cannot handle the energy that comes with winning millions. The lottery winner finds that it enhanced all their unconscious beliefs, and they lose all the money. In fact, most lottery winners say that it was a curse rather than a blessing.

Money or the achievement of materialistic items only offer a temporary happiness. It is never lasting. It is fleeting and the search for more continues again. Think about all things you have accumulated over the years. How about all the gifts you received for holidays and birthdays throughout your life? In the moment, they felt euphoric and fulfilling. They brought happiness and a smile to your face in the moment. In the end, they lose their value, or they are just not as fulfilling. Most of the stuff gets trashed, sits in the closet collecting dust, or is just not important anymore. We continue to search for something outside of us to bring us happiness. The external is always changing and will always be fleeting.

Even the physical body can be of a materialistic endeavor. It is of temporary satisfaction and fulfillment should you place your focus and value on it. Your physical body only lasts so long. To place your value and worth on body image can only bring temporary happiness but in the end it will lead to suffering as long as you are attached to it.

The material search is endless because it is outside of yourself. It focuses your fulfillment on the external world. That which is outside of you cannot fulfill the emptiness that is inside of you. You think millions of dollars will make you happy? You think the new car or big home will bring you peace? Not a chance. It can certainly ease the root chakra imbalanced energy issues, but you will find all that energy will be distorted in the other chakras. If you were not happy before you had it, then you will likely be unhappy after.

The physical materialism of our existence should be used to enhance our spiritual growth. To enhance our ability to love and further understand ourselves as Source. Unfortunately, we have been taught that materialism is the sole purpose of our existence. It is a hamster wheel of fleeting happiness.

Physical manifestation of goods or services naturally comes with spiritual growth. Abundance is naturally felt when you open to Source and allow the flow of Source energy to move through you unrestricted. What I can say is as you work through the distortions in your energy field, you are increasing or allowing Source energy to flow more freely. The will of Source can flow like a clear river. The greater the flow of Source energy through you, the greater the magnetic force for abundance. The sheer ability to work on oneself, to love oneself more, will ultimately lead to more abundance. Via the law of attraction, you will increase the confirmation of your self-love in your external experience. It will naturally increase your abundance and materialistic desires.

Life is charged like electricity. This life substance exists in electrical suspension until something exerts force on it. Without intention there is no effect. You will manifest effortlessly when you are able to direct that life force with full embodiment and full awareness of Source. You will be able to direct the electricity of life through you as the creator.

# CHAPTER 9:
# LEAD BY EXAMPLE

In a gold glittering ink, my spirit guide wrote down her name. It was in cursive and the ink looked like it was alive. There was a scintillating golden light that flowed through the ink and the written letters of her name glowed. I could not get the image out of my head. It was her way of introducing herself to me so that I would remember it. An introduction so that I would know it was not just my imagination. I remember the fairness of her skin and her blonde hair. I also remember the beautiful rainbow aura that surrounded her. We discussed many things in our meeting together. Much of it has brought me to where I am today.

I could sense our time together was ending. We got up from where we were sitting outside and moved into an entryway. I began to hear a song playing. I cannot recall the name of the band or who wrote the song. I only remember it had a strong familiarity to it, like an old rock anthem. I looked down from where it was playing from and saw the phrase: *Lead by Example.*

It has taken me some time grasp the totality of this simple phrase. Lead by example. These three words are almost elementary. As if you could see them written or hanging on the wall of a classroom. Words to live by. It has the same ring of divinity as the golden rule: *Treat people the way you want to be treated.* It feels timeless. Lead by example.

The interaction with my guide left me a bit shocked and in wonderment. I felt a tremendous task at hand, without much of a clue as to how to accomplish it. The experience left me with a burning question in my mind. In the days that followed I asked myself, "By what example am I supposed to lead?" I had no clue as to what the example should be. It has taken me some time to understand what the example is.

It has taken my entire healing process and spiritual journey, up until this point, to understand what my spirit guide was trying to get me to understand about being an example. That example is by the way I live. I am to be a living example of a path to reconnect with Source. A reflection for others to see Source within themselves by living my authentic self. To be a living reminder of what they have forgotten. To live my life as an empowered and sovereign Source being. An example of remembering that I am Source.

These are my experiences of finding Source within me. It has been my way to finding more peace and joy in my life. It is my example for you to use if you so choose to. I can only offer this path of self-discovery so that you can find your own healing and empowerment. For I can only lead by my examples, my experiences, and my own energetic vibration. This is not the only path. It is one of many to embody as you create your own. These written words are my vibrational example by which I lead. In hopes that you take on the torch and find your true self as well. In turn, that you become a living example for others.

What does it truly mean to lead by example? You hear it all the time. The gravity of this phrase is far greater and impressive than you can imagine. The nature of leading by example is a full embodiment of what you believe to be true. You are a living, walking, breathing, and vibrationally expression of that truth. A beacon for others to learn from. It encompasses all that you are. Your way of being is the example. You become a portal for people to walk through to access a vibrational experience.

I write these words with an energetic intention of providing you the choice of empowerment and love. An intention to help you remember Source love. To help you rediscover yourself as a beloved creator and to acknowledge where that power comes from. It lays within you and can never be taken away. The intention to provide a path to oneness, to Source through my experience.

To lead by example is to live it. To live with the energy coursing through every fiber of your being. A continued and dedicated practice to love through self-discovery. This is a lifestyle by which we choose to peer ever so deep into ourselves. It becomes natural to jump into the cauldrons of pressure and heat that are the transmutative fires of self-love. This is the choice of the warrior to face their demons with courage and strength. It is only through practice and consistency that one develops the natural tendencies to embody awareness and clarity.

Undoubtedly, you will become frustrated and tested within your own life and journey. You will ultimately be led to experience all the rejected pieces of yourself. That is the way. To feel whole is to accept the rejected pieces of yourself. It will be painful to look directly into the mirror and see what you have become. There will be times you will want to give up and go no further, but your higher self will urge you on. It knows your pain is the doorway to feeling whole again. Forever onward you will be called forth by the depths of your being. It is Source urging you to know yourself more. Forever onward you will move to rediscover yourself.

You will become the vibration state of being that people are seeking. People will be looking for Source connection. People are desperate to find their connection to Source love. In this cycle of time, there is a tremendous yearning to feel loved again. Your vibration and your energy will be their reminder. You will be their example by which they can find more joy, love, and peace in their lives. It is through you, that you will offer the choice of healing. It will be through you that you can help others see their true selves. To see past the illusions of separation and drop the heaviness that burdens them. It will be through you that a great catalyst will occur for others to seek inward. It will be through you that others will awaken to the choice of love over fear.

Lead by embodying Source love throughout your entire being, your entire essence. Lead through your openness to be true to yourself. The acceptance of what you are becomes authentic. Your authenticity will be the way. It will lead you to your higher self that awaits patiently on the other side. Your higher self will free you from the projections of others and the shackles of fear that have kept you small and little. Free yourself from these illusions that keep you from feeling peace, joy, and happiness in your life.

Your higher self is the truth of what you are. You are part of Source, and you are a creator. The more you work on yourself the clearer the conduit you will become for Source. You will become a clear flowing radiant river of Source energy. It will radiate to anyone and everyone that you come in contact with. Whether they know it or not, your vibration will shift them. Your vibration will be embedded within their energy field and a shift will occur.

Through you is how you show the world what change can be. For you *ARE* the change. You are the change you have been waiting for. To affect change does not mean to tell people what to do. It is merely to show them the example, to show them the way. It is to offer insight through your way of being without judgement to them. To show them doors that they may not be able to see. Lead by example is to see their divinity and to see their perfection as you extend the hand of love.

Many, however, will reject it. Many will refuse it because they fear it. They fear seeing their own selves and how they have unconsciously created. They refuse to see the weights they carry. Denial of the burdens they hold. Refusal to see their reality crumble to the weight of the truth. Honor them. Love them for their choice and remain in your light.

## VIBRATION CREATES CHANGE

There can be times that we can feel small, insignificant, and powerless to change our lives and even more so when it comes to changing the world. This can feel especially true when the world seems so chaotic and tumultuous. There exists a relentless amount of humanitarian issues. There is starvation, war, and other inhumane experiences that we would prefer to be otherwise. One may look upon that which they experience and ask, "I am just one. How can I affect such a change?" The only power and control you have is what is done through you. The smallest change in vibration can have an exponential impact.

History has shown how one human's actions can change the world. Through their being they were able to move masses. Martin Luther King, Jr. created a change for civil rights in the United States. Mahatma Gandhi affected change for the entire country of India. Stalin and Hitler had the same effect, but with much different outcomes. The point is that individuals can make changes. It can happen and it does happen. Everyday people are affecting the course of our collective experience and the world. It is done through the portal that is the individual, the creator.

When you stand within your power, you can change the world. For the world is but the macrocosm of what is within you. The start to change does not come from unconscious reactions. It does not come from external forces only. It must also come from inner forces as well. It comes from inspired actions of love.

Your ability to love yourself is the start. Self-love is a vibration far stronger than the rampant fear in our lives. Self-love is the starting point to break the darkness that holds people in self-imposed prisons. Love will overpower and cause a catalyst for change far greater than you can imagine.

There is an old analogy about self-love and how it can offer healing to the world. Imagine that there are two cups. One cup represents you and the other cup is someone else. Working on yourself and loving yourself is like pouring water into your own cup. As you continue to love and heal, you continue to pour the water into your cup. Your cup with become full and will eventually spill over. The over running water will spill into the other cup as you naturally continue to fill your own cup up.

Your ability to provide love to yourself will eventually pour over onto other people. Your love will spill outwardly and help fill other people's cups. This is because you are a living, walking aspect of love. It becomes you and you can effortlessly provide it. It will be a pure untainted love that can be shared with anyone willing to accept it.

You cannot provide love to someone effortlessly and unconditionally without working on yourself. Otherwise, it is a distortion or a depletion of your own self. The well of unlimited love only comes from within, not from an outwardly projection. You must love yourself first so deeply and so immensely, that your love expands beyond you naturally. Become complete and whole within yourself and reflect that vibrational state to others so that they may see what peace, love, and joy is. Radiate through your being what an example of the divine light that is Source love to catalyze others.

Much like the cup analogy, you cannot control whether someone wants their cup filled. It is an illusion to think otherwise. Sure, you can force a choice on someone, but that choice is ultimately theirs to make. It is still within their control and not yours. You cannot change people or force people to change their minds. You can only catalyze by showing them through your example.

The only control you have is how you create and hold your vibration. Nothing more and nothing less. You can bring a horse to a watering hole, but you cannot make it drink the water. Why spend so much energy in trying to make a resisting horse drink water? It is not your job to make them drink. This is particularly true when it comes to healing. Healing can only be done through the individual. Healing does not come from you. Healing comes through the choice of the individual to heal themselves. A healer can only show the way to be healed. The individual must make the choice to be healed. If they do not choose to listen, it is their own free will. It is always their choice. We are to only extend our hand and show them if they so choose.

Our experience on this planet is such that we may never see an end to suffering. It is made to be that way. It is the experience that we yearn for. We must be able to find the love in each choice and in each moment. Love can always be found. Source is in all.

I discussed the identity of the divine energies running through you in Chapter 4. The divine feminine energies and the divine masculine energies are imbalanced in many ways. We have focused our energy primarily in the divine masculine energies which has led to imbalance in our creations. An imbalance that has created results which have only repressed energies. It has repressed people, it has repressed emotions, and it has disempowered people and further escalate social issues.

Think about human history and the major themes we continue to revisit as a society. It seems history repeats itself even though we have felt we resolved these issues. Who would think we would still be dealing with human trafficking, wars, human rights, slavery, racism, etc.? What type of energy has been used for "solving" these things? Imbalance focuses on the divine masculine energy. Protesting, fighting, conquering, and force. Fighting fire with fire as they would say. Fire only burns, scorching both users and the landscape the battle occurs on. Water is needed to subdue the flames. When energy is forcefully repressed, it will continue to fight its way out. It will show itself in a myriad of ways. Are we not destined to relive old human patterns if we continue to repress people and their emotions? History repeats itself because we have not learned our lessons about separation.

How about our Mother Earth? On a far larger scale, we feel so separate from this planet even though we exist on it. We are born of it and from it. We are deeply dependent on the resources and unconditional love that our Mother Earth provides. We use every element found on her to survive and thrive. We are integral to her as she is to us. Even our breath is part of the natural cycle of life here. We breathe in oxygen that the plants exhale. The plants harness the carbon dioxide that we exhale. Yet, we continue to see ourselves as separate from our own place of birth. Driven by imbalanced energies of creation that wreak havoc within our own existence, unable to live in harmony.

Now think about yourself as the individual. For the collective would not experience these things if the individual did not hold the same energy. As above so below, as within so without. We are all individually adding to the collective. What the collective shows us is the macro of the micro within us. The individual has unconsciously treated themselves as separate and broken. Within are the pieces that are divided, separated, and rejected from the whole. We go about our lives avoiding these aspects of ourselves and creating realities that are fundamentally based on that energy. How have you gone about dealing with these collective experiences within your personal life? What beliefs and emotions are brought forward from the experience? Are you recreating from the macro the same experience in a more personal setting?

We must become whole within ourselves should we want to heal what we see in our external human collective. We must look at ourselves first before we try to change the external. For the doorway to change is not through forcing on to another. We have seen time and time again that it does not work out when you force change. One must accept the decision for themselves. We must become responsible for our lives and the choices we make. The doorway for change is through the individual. Change does not occur when you give the power to someone else. How much change in your life occurred because of someone else? Let us take the president of the United States. How much of your life has really changed because of the president? Someone like the president may have an external indirect influence, but someone as powerful as the president has little impact on your life directly. The biggest change I have seen for anyone is when they choose to make the change for themselves. The biggest life changes occur when someone decides they want a better life, or that they want to be healthier, and they take action to do so. They take ownership and responsibility for their creations and choose differently. They choose to direct their energy in a focus that betters their lives. The individual directly impacts their own life. The biggest shifts in my life came when I decided to change. My peace and happiness did not come from someone telling me that I was unhappy and that I needed to change. It came when I chose to do it. I took charge of my life and made that decision for myself. Change was brought through me and my own being. I became the change that I wanted to see. When I changed who I was, then my external reality shifted to match what was inside of me.

Mahatma Gandhi said, "Be the change you wish to see in the world." You must become what you desire to see in the world. You must become the change. When the individual accepts the responsibility of their life and they decide they will be what they want to see is when things change. The start is within the empowered individual. We can empower ourselves and become the change for other people to witness. It starts with you working on yourself to become conscious of your vibration. To become aware of how you are putting your vibration out into the world. Change comes from within and only through the individual.

If the empowered individual chooses not to, then the choice is theirs to make. We cannot force others to change because we cannot control their decisions. It must be theirs to make. For instance, let us take the concept of social injustice. There are several issues with trying to force change with social injustice. The first is you as the creator believe there is injustice. You have embodied the energy of injustice or victimhood. A choice by which you have placed your intention and judgement into. This could be because of underlying repressed traumas or emotions that make you feel like a victim and that there is social injustice. A belief has been established. The second issue is you as the creator are trying to correct injustice through force upon another. You are repressing your own energies and repressing the energies of another. We all know by now that this will only perpetuate the reality surrounding injustice. Lastly, you as the creator are denying the experience of another creator. You are rejecting the experience of another creator that may be desiring to experience injustice. Who are you to judge Source creation? You are not the only Source creator out there.

The belief in injustice will spur the Universe into action. It will spring forth by intention based on the choice to judge. You have created an experience through fear. By giving energy and awareness to an injustice, it will continue to manifest and maintain the vibratory timeline in which you are experiencing it. It will maintain the reality until such time the creator deems it no longer serves them. The more fuel or energy you put into it, the more it runs. The injustice continues because creators wish it to be seen. It is so because you deem it to be so. In a co-created experience, we also must acknowledge that the other creator is creating injustice for themselves. Remember, you are not the only creator. Are their desires and experiences not divine as well as yours? Why should another creator's creation be rejected?

The challenge is to find the love within the injustice. Can you find a higher perspective that is aware of the divinity playing the illusionary game of separation? There is love to be seen here. Is there not a higher form of love than of service for another? Love is another creator saying to you, "I will be of service for you, so that you may experience your desire of separation. In doing so, I offer my love by becoming what you will hate so that you may experience more of yourself."

## LOVE IS HEALING

Your pain and traumas occurred at a level of consciousness that is deeply embedded in separation. It is because of separation that you feel hurt, pain, betrayal, unloved, and unworthy. It occurs because of the vibrational match to the identity of separation. When you feel separate, you feel duality and polarity. You are either rejecting or accepting your experiences in your life as part of you or not. The illusion of separation lends itself to hurting another.

Think about your life. Every aspect of our reality feels separate from one another. We feel separate from every other human. We feel separate from this planet. We feel separate from the animal kingdom and the plant kingdom. It is laughable to think that we continue to destroy our lands and forests in complete ignorance to the fact we rely on nature to survive. We feel separate in many ways. We fall for illusions, separation by towns, sports, gender, culture, politics, ethnicity, wealth, education, etc., the list goes on. That which we do not accept as part of us we reject.

When we continue to reject our reality, we continue to manifest realities that mirror it back to us. We perpetuate the pain and suffering in our world because we are rejecting ourselves. We continue to create from the same vibrational state that created the pain. You must rise above the frequency of separation and find love. Love is the healing way.

Love is the higher healing vibration. It is a vibration of wholeness. Love is the only way to heal and is a higher vibration than fear. Love is returning to one and finding unity. It removes the distortions that fear energy creates, which is separation. Separation created all the suffering you are experiencing. You must rise above and beyond the separation that created the rejection to heal. Healing occurs at a level of love.

How do we heal a physical wound? Do you reject the wound and continue as nothing happened? Do you try to heal the wound by doing the exact same things that created the wound? No. You must rest, you must bandage it, you must tend to it and allow it to be healed. You must love it. You must offer the space for it to heal by accepting it and loving it as such.

Think about when a child gets hurt and begins to cry. What does the child do? The child seeks their mother. Their mother offers compassion and love. She holds them in comfort and seeks to ease their pain. The closest to Source love is that of a mother's love. We must find that love for ourselves so that we can heal. We must offer ourselves love first by openly embracing our pain and suffering that has long been hidden in the dark. Love allows, expresses, and accepts the dark, and together it rises above the level on which it was created.

To heal is to rise above the pain and say, "I no longer reject myself. I no longer hold on to pain and hurt. I choose to honor my feelings. I choose to accept this part of me I have rejected." In doing so you become whole. Wholeness accepts all that you are and brings peace. It is harmony. You will find your power within that harmony and raise your vibration to a state of love.

The primary focus of this material is on patterns that we are trying to avoid. As you move through your journey, you will find more joy and love for life as well. I assure you that there is so much more love in life as you continue your spiritual and healing journey. You will become aware of the bounty of beauty and love that existed all around you that you have been blind to. It will be as if heaven was right there in front of you and a veil was removed from you. The immense joy that can be found in any moment is just a vibration away.

## THE GOLDEN ONES

I remember a meeting with a spirit where I was called a "golden one." Not to say that *I* was the golden one, but rather humanity itself was the golden one. The color gold is associated with compassion, selflessness, purity, altruism, protection, regality, holiness, and divinity. Think about the many images of golden halos found around saints, angels, or any other divinely anointed being. There is a golden halo, or aura that surrounds those beings because of the compassion and service they offer to others. It is through great wisdom, knowledge, and experiences that one attains a golden hue and can be a symbol of love and compassion.

In a sense, humanity will become the golden ones. You are becoming golden through this life. You are in a grand experiment or a great lesson. A deepening and exploration of love in such a way that our world could be called a school. A school where heavy densities, low vibrations, extreme ranges of emotions, and feelings so disconnected from Source are common. What a learning experience for us to incarnate into this place! Think about the knowledge and wisdom gained from this place and how your expansion can assist others. We are experiencing such depth of separation and yet we overcome it all. We feel so far apart from Source and we still find our way back to Source again.

The immeasurable value that you gain from this human experience can be of benefit to others. You will be able to integrate the extremes of your emotions to assist others. It is through integrating your emotions that you will offer great benefit for another. To be able to manage the densities and honor extremes that are anger and love will be why you are a golden one. You will be golden with wisdom and compassion. Golden for your ability to find love even with such adversities.

The golden one finds the strength, courage, and love to face their fears and heal what needs to be healed. They take up the action of self-love and allow what has been hidden to move into the light. To honor it and move forward. The more you work on yourself the more you remove the limited distortions that keep you small and little. Each step of awareness and self-love will only empower you and help you see past illusions that no longer serve you. It will clear your energy field and expand outwardly in radiant love energy.

Your beliefs will shift, and you will find more joy and happiness in your life. You will heal yourself of old patterns and release repressed emotions that are diseasing your body. You will naturally heal your karma and your ancestral karma through the action of self-love. Things will move and change to reflect what you are becoming. Through your love and compassion, you will find new relationships, new opportunities, new love, and a new you. It starts with you. It starts with living the way you want to. To honor yourself and follow what is true for you. You become authentic and align with your higher self.

What happens when you turn a light on in the dark? It shines and illuminates everything. Even the smallest light can illuminate an entire room. Be that light. Live YOUR life. Not ruled by others, not ruled by fear, but ruled by your own love. Be a clear conduit for the will of Source to know itself through love. Let it flow unrestricted and unabated. Release the fear and lead through constant love and compassion for yourself. It will be a state of being that you will be able to hold space that others need. They will find you and be reminded of what they are through you. It will catalyze them to find their own divinity because you are the golden one. Sovereign and golden you will stand within humanity as a beacon of light for those who need to find joy, peace, and connection in their lives. Through your authentic and empowered self, you will be able to affect change and shine light where it needs to shine.

Your light may scare others as well. They will judge you and project their fears onto you. You may not feel like you belong here because of that. You may feel different and feel like an outcast. Many of you may have the desire to leave, but that too is an illusion. I assure you that you are meant to be here. You are exactly where you need to be. You are here to change this world. Not to assimilate into it. Your energy, your vibration is here to affect change.

That difference within you will create change. People will see something different about you. They will wonder how you remain so happy and peaceful while such chaos swirls around you. You will become the eye of the hurricane. You will be the center, the calmness amongst the destructive forces spiraling around in the outside world. The vibrational calmness and gentleness will be the shelter that they seek from their own storm. It will naturally attract people. They will be drawn into the golden purity of your light.

## THE GOLDEN AGE OF HUMANITY

All things in life have a cycle. There are cycles to our human experience and there are cycles we experience beyond our human container. We experience certain themes within each part of a cycle.

Take the planet Earth and the seasons we experience. Each season has a certain characteristic and theme that plays out. Spring is about growth, new beginnings, and rebirth. The sun stays in the sky longer and warmth returns and melts the snow and ice. Whereas the season of fall is a time about harvesting the crops. The weather turns colder, and the days get shorter. Plants begin to wilt and die off. Animals start to get ready for winter and migration begins. It is about understanding our growth and taking away the lessons from our experiences. Summer and winter have themes as well. The point is that there are overall themes to each season or cycle to life. It would be of interest to discern the times or the cycles that you are in.

According to astrology, the last two thousand years were called the Age of Pisces. We have moved out of the Age of Pisces. The Age of Pisces is associated with hardships, sacrifice, faith, beliefs, and struggle. The symbol for Pisces is two fish swimming in opposite directions tied to one another. It is representative of polarity and duality conjoined together by these two fish. The lessons we have learned here are carried into the next cycle, the Age of Aquarius.

The Age of Aquarius is a sign for humanitarianism with ideals for the greater good of all. Utopia or paradise-like visions in which the individual will find more in common than different with one another. It is a time of connection and joining together as one in unity. The sign for Aquarius is about hope and the future. The symbol used for Aquarius is a water bearer. It is a human pouring water that flows freely and equally to all. This can be seen as abundance or truth as it flows out to all.

Like all things in life, there are cycles to life. We experience certain themes within each part of a cycle or period of time. What befell us in the Age of Pisces will be the opposite in the Age of Aquarius. We must then experience a time or cycle of rejuvenation. A time of abundance and relaxation. A time of great advancement in technology and humanitarian accomplishments. This is the golden age of humanity.

This planet has been deeply embedded in an energy that has felt stuck and heavy. It is a reflection of the consciousness that has existed here for more than a millennium. It is reflective of the Age of Pisces. The overall consciousness of this planet has been unconscious, imbalanced, and repressive. It is deeply embedded in creations of polarity and duality which cause great hardships and struggles. This can be seen everywhere in a macro sense. We can see these characteristics within our societal structures of the health care system, the financial system, the education system, and the political structure. We are constantly waging wars, dealing with the lack of resources, geopolitical tension, etc. The characteristics are reflective of the individual as well. Individually, we hold on to deeply repressed emotions and energies that create polarity and duality. People are struggling and dealing with hardships on a level not seen before. People attack one another because they feel separated and fearful. The vibrational frequency of this planet and consciousness is low and dense, but people are waking up. They are hearing the call from Source to wake up and remember who they truly are. This is shifting the energy on this planet, and many are feeling something different.

The move into the golden age of humanity will not come without drama. The energies are shifting and what we know of the old guard fights hard to stay alive. The old guard energy is deeply embedded within all of us and there can be such a dissonance when integrating a new higher vibration.

Cymatics is the process of making sounds we hear into a visible expression.

They use different mediums, such as sand, for sounds to transmit their vibration and the results are incredible physical displays of patterns of sand. The interesting thing to notice is what happens when you change from one vibration to another. The original pattern of sand becomes unstable, and chaos ensues. Sand goes everywhere and there is no resemblance of before. The pattern gets destroyed as the vibration shifts to the next resonance. When it reaches the next resonance, the sand begins to arrange itself. As the resonance or vibration is reached and held, a new form or a new structure of pattern is revealed.

This is exactly what is happening to everything on this planet. It is a recalibration to something new. The drama that will play out through this shift will certainly feel like the end of the world. It is because it is the end of one energy or vibration and it is the beginning of a new one. It is the end of a vibrational reality that no longer serves humanity into a new vibrational reality that aligns with more Source connection.

Many will feel the urge to raise their vibrations to match the new energy. Many will wake up from their unconscious slumber and realize this is not the way to live. They will awaken in a remembrance of what they are. It will create such discord between their old self and their new self. There will be a relentlessness to this energy as people fight against themselves. People will feel their illusions within the old energy start to collapse. They will feel extremes in polarity and duality. It will become an emotional rollercoaster for many which will lead to irrational behavior and craziness. The shift is a full destruction and restructuring of what we have known. This is all to catalyze us into awareness. All of this is to catalyze us to seek Source within. Inward is the way out and the answers to what we seek. Inward is how to rebalance energies within us. The key to peace is to reconnect with the truth. We are Source and we have never been separated. Become the creator and feel oneness.

## Golden Human Exercise:

*Get into a meditative state. When you feel ready, begin to envision what it would be like to live in the golden age of humanity. Imagine what utopia would feel like to you. What kinds of systems are in place? What would you be doing? What freedoms would you have? What would the world be like if you had free energy? What would it look like if we lived in harmony with the earth? What kind of relationships would we have? Travel or space exploration? Connections with other dimensions?*

*Enjoy your time in this space.*

## ONENESS

I wrote this book with the intention of there being nine chapters. Each chapter representing a number relating to your journey. In numerology, the number one is the starting point and is associated with new beginnings. This is a new beginning for you, but it is also the closure of another, the ending of the old you. The number nine represents completion. It represents selflessness and compassion. Nine is associated with universal love and the desire to be of service to others. In many ways, this represents the end of your journey with this material but also a new beginning. For the beginning and the end are the same. You will find there are many paradoxes in life because we are a paradox as well. Source is all knowing but seeks to understand itself. Why would an all knowing being seek to understand itself? This is the paradox we exist in. Another paradox is knowing we are Source, whole and complete, but we are also only a fragment of Source. You feel separate but you are always connected. You feel unworthy, but you are already worthy. You live in an infinite Universe, but you limit the Universe. We are moving to a consciousness that can hold both at the same time. We can understand that both can be true and are perfectly acceptable.

You are moving your consciousness from a limited human perspective to one that is far broader and far more encompassing. You are moving your consciousness to a place where it can hold a perspective that is beyond just your linear self. You are moving toward a space where you can hold multidimensionality. You can hold consciousness and perspectives that are more quantum. It is the end of linearity into the consciousness of the quantum and multidimensional self. You are starting to see that you are everywhere, past, present, and future. You are here and now within all that there is, and you hold all the potentials within you. This awareness is moving you upwards and outwards.

In a sense, you could say that we are moving up from the lower physically focused chakras, of the root, sacral, and solar plexus. You are moving into the heart chakra and up. Your consciousness has evolved enough to move beyond the physical self and the ego. You are moving beyond physically focused energy centers into the more etheric-like energy centers of the heart, throat, third eye, and crown chakras. You are moving toward Source connection, multidimensionality, truth, and love in all.

The heart chakra is the beginning of this transition. It is unconditional love for all. The heart is also associated with acceptance. It ties all the lower three chakras together through acceptance and love. You can accept what you see in your reality and find the love of the one and infinite creator that is Source. All is Source and you are Source.

You can sense Source is everywhere and everything in the heart chakra. With an evolved consciousness you see with love. You begin to understand that we are all part of one. You see past the illusion that keeps you limited and fearful. The illusion of separation distorts Source love and makes you fear another.

You begin to understand that we are all loved divine creators. Everyone is just like yourself, a creator, seeking to understand themselves through their own experiences. Some are more fixated in the human journey compared to others, but it does not make it any worse or better. It just is. Their journey may be to fully experience the human separation. Perhaps, they have chosen not to find Source within themselves this lifetime. Your journey has led you here. A journey of self-awareness and self-healing to bring you back to Source. There is no reason to judge another for their choices on their own journey.

The desire to judge another for their actions is less needed. You can sense there is more to each person you encounter. You can be compassionate toward others because they are you experiencing themselves through their lives. What is there to judge when you can see yourself in all? For you are aware that another divine being is experiencing themselves through their own choice and will. It is their choice to create their experiences. We all have divine choices to create. You can see the divinity in everything and can appreciate our differences. The concept of separation becomes less of a focus and fades. The perspective of hating another for their skin color, their wealth, their culture, their country, their clothes, etc., begins to shift. We lose the desire to experience ourselves through the illusions. We move our consciousness higher and see through the eyes of oneness. Oneness can be understanding of all differences. You can be compassionate of other creators' choices knowing that we are all Source experiencing ourselves through the multidimensionality of itself. We may be able to heal our divisions and differences through our connection of Source.

This shift to oneness will force you to become whole as well. You will feel an unease in your energy as the rejected aspect of you begins to stir and move. You will feel the repressed energies begin to bubble up into your reality. Emotions that were once rejected by you will manifest and come forward to be loved by you. You will be forced to look at them. There are energies accelerating on many levels. There is a quickening to your awareness and to the energies you hold on to. It will become evident that you are spiraling through each circle of the flower of life pattern at a rate not seen before. The time afforded to work through your patterns will shorten because the new energy vibration is higher. It may feel like you are dealing with the many patterns at once rather than one at a time. Some may experience instant manifestations of patterns at an elevated pace. It will be a crash course for emotional healing and balance for many. This is all for your highest good.

The vibrational environment we are experiencing in our daily lives is ever so increasing. It is like being in a dark room and the lights are slowly getting brighter. You must adjust to it or you will have some difficulty keeping up with the energy. You must adjust and raise your vibrations. The vibrational differences of energy will cause disturbances within you. The energies will seek to rebalance to the higher vibrational resonance. Energy likes to move from low to high in a hierarchical sense. Your dense traumas and patterns will be most prevalent going forward. It will be those things you reject about yourself that will brutally confront you. You will stand face-to-face with yourself with no other option except to make peace. There is no more fence sitting as they say. You will not be able to have one foot in the old you and one foot in the new you. The convenience of time to integrate your rejected self has expired and you will need to take action.

The action of self-love is needed. It is only through you that life can be better. If not you, then who else? Who else can fulfill the void within you? Who else is going to be responsible for your life? There is no one else that can do it but you, so stop running from yourself. Stop saying you are not worthy of it. Stop fearing yourself and give yourself the commitment to change for the better. It is only by your hand that you will find what you want. The action of self-love and honoring your rejected fragments is what brings peace. You will never regret the love you offer yourself.

Everything outlined in this guide is to help you move with the grand wave. It is to help you shift your consciousness toward love. This will help you keep afloat and move with ease through a potentially difficult transition for humanity. Alleviate the pressures from the higher vibrations by releasing the heavy densities you are carrying. That can only occur through love of self. It does not occur fearing yourself.

The creator who chooses to act with fear will experience the opposite. The energies will become increasingly more catalytic. Those that choose not to become one with Source will feel the impeding pressures of life. Their world will begin to close in on them. Life will become more intense as they continue their judgements of fear. Further and further into the chaos until nothing remains. It will only change when they chose to turn toward their Source connection. Only inward will they find the keys to their kingdom.

Humanity is raising its consciousness. It is moving beyond the individual human container and moving toward a more quantum consciousness. More and more people are anchoring this consciousness on our planet than ever before. They are beginning to see themselves not only as individuals, but also that we are all connected as divine beings from Source. This higher level of connection is seen through the eyes of the creator and will bring you to oneness. You will find a deeper connection with your emotions, your body, your relationships, your experiences, and all that is within your world. A renewed sense of self that is more grounded to life and is more peaceful.

Peace may not come to us as a collective the way you desire, but that does not mean you cannot have peace for yourself. Oneness does not mean you have to follow along with the chaos of the collective. Oneness does not mean you have to become what others are. You can be peaceful and exist along with the chaos of the world. It can be both. You may walk with such joy in your heart while others suffer deeply within their own lives. Be compassionate to their divine choice. Allow them to experience what they need to find connection to Source without judgement. Be an example of oneness. Show them peace.

During one of my runs around my neighborhood, I came upon a bird. It was mid-day, and the sun was shining brightly high in the sky. The bird was staring at its own reflection in the window of a house. It began to aggressively flap its wings and proceeded to peck at its own reflection. There was loud tapping and scratching as the bird attacked. It was acting as if it was defending its territory. The bird began a full-scale assault upon the window, mistaking its own reflection as another threatening bird.

I wondered how the bird would have reacted differently if it realized the truth of what it saw. Would it have given up on the idea of attacking itself? Would it have recognized the fault of its actions? Would the bird have admired the beauty in the reflection? Most likely, it would have paid no attention and moved on.

From a perspective of oneness, you can see other creators acting the same as the bird. People pecking and attacking at their own reflection not knowing the truth of their illusion. How differently would you approach a conflict situation if you knew that other people were just a reflection? How different would you talk and treat the people across from you? Could you see yourself in everyone that you meet? What kind of love can be found when you look into another's eyes and see the one Source creator? Would you see their faults with kindness and compassion? What peace can be brought about if we could all see ourselves within each other? The peace we desire can be here and now. You do not have to wait for it. It can occur when you deeply connect with who you are and what you are. Peace can come when you can connect with Source within and see through the eyes of the creator. The creator sees the divinity in all. It sees love in all. Can you look at your neighbor and see love? Can you look at a stranger and see love? Can you find love in those that do you wrong? Can you find love in the suffering of others? Can you find love in the dying patient? Can you find love in the inhuman events? Can you find love within yourself? Source love can be found in any moment. It can be found when you move beyond the human self. It can be found when you understand that everyone comes from the same energy. When you find it, you will be able to look into your enemy's eyes and see yourself. You will see yourself and the service of love being offered. That is when peace can be attained within you.

This journey has been recollecting the pieces of you that were given away and forgotten about. In a sense, this was a journey of remembering what you are. A rediscovery process to becoming the creator that you have always been. To remember that you are and have always been powerful. You are never a victim. Life does not happen to you. Life happens because of you.

You know the truth. The truth of what you are. You are Source. You are connected to all, and all is connected to you. Source creates through you, and you are more loved that you will ever know. You are whole and complete. You are the change you are waiting for. You are your own savior. You are free to create the life that you desire. Create it because you are the creator.

I bless you, my dear soul family. I honor you with great love and affection for being who you are. I am grateful for your co-creation with me in this moment. May the light of Source shine brightly within you. May Source assist you in life. May you always come to know how deeply loved you are.

And so it is.

# ACKNOWLEDGEMENTS

I have found that we are not meant to do everything alone. We need each other to expand our energy, to know ourselves, and to share our love. My desire to write this material and to know myself could not have come about without others, and I would not be where I am today without them. I would like to acknowledge the joy and the immense gratitude for their participation in my life.

First and foremost, I am grateful to Source for creating all the beauty and joy that is my life.

I would like to acknowledge my loving and caring father and mother, Gregory and Lauren Lemay, for their unwavering love and support. I have such a deep gratitude for their acceptance and for giving me the foundation to grow and to thrive.

I would like to acknowledge my sisters for their support and openness. Thank you for being there when I desperately needed someone to talk to. Thank you for your support and love. Thank you to my brother, for being who he is.

I would like to acknowledge my wife, Jessica, for her love and commitment in my life. Her compassion, patience, and support for me through my spiritual awakening and journey was everything. She was willing to change and grow with me. I am grateful the Universe brought her to me. She has been my rock as well as the rock of our family. Thank you for keeping my spirits up and helping me believe in myself.

I would like to acknowledge my children. I am honored to have you in my life more than you will ever know. Thank you for coming into my life and awakening me. Thank you for teaching me every day and pushing me to love myself more than I could understand.

I would like to acknowledge my biological parents, but especially my mother Keo. I am thankful for her love and the sacrifices she made for me.

I would like to acknowledge all the beautiful souls who have guided me along my path. My amazing soul family of friends that have listened to me and helped me. A great honor to my spirit guides for their love and all they have shown me on my journey.

CPSIA information can be obtained
at www.ICGtesting.com
Printed in the USA
BVHW070759221221
624594BV00009B/526

9 781737 628798